# ACT OF
# GOD

# ACT OF
# GOD

M. LEANNE TODD

**ARPress**
ILLUMINATING IDEAS
EMPOWERING VOICES

**ARPress**
45 Dan Road Suite 5
Canton MA 02021

Hotline: 1(888) 821-0229
Fax:      1(508) 545-7580

Ordering Information:
Quantity sales. Special discounts are available on quantity purchases by corporations, associations, and others. For details, contact the publisher at the address above.

Printed in the United States of America.

| ISBN-13: | Softcover | 979-8-89389-168-3 |
| | eBook | 979-8-89389-167-6 |

Library of Congress Control Number: 2024914623

# CONTENTS

# FOREWORD

If anyone comes speaking in the name of the LORD Jesus Christ, it is imperative that their lives become an open book. That is because having intimate knowledge of the author's life allows people to have a better perspective and sense of discernment about what is written. For this reason, I feel it necessary to share not only about the strength of my faith with the reader of this collection, but also... about my *weakness*.

I was diagnosed with bipolar disorder at a young age in life – my 9th grade year in high school. One day I began to physically shake in my gym class. I don't remember that. I only remember being escorted to the school office, where the general consensus was that I had been "doing drugs." There I suffered a brief interrogation about my would-be drug connections, for which I had no coherent answers.

I sat, bracing for the impending wrath of a militant anti-drug regime and whatever authorities would be called...you know, for BACK UP, against this wily and decidedly *baked* honor roll student. Fortunately, only my mother was called. She could be plenty frightening in her own rite, but at least she didn't carry a gun— usually. (You must realize, this all happened in Texas. And Texas is a state where signs forbidding firearms must be posted on the doorsteps of convalescent homes.)

Eventually I was taken to the local emergency room, and from there I was ultimately sent to a hospital cities away from home. I would spend the next few months in that private hospital which focused on treating various conditions in adolescents such as: substance abuse, mental illnesses, eating disorders, and so forth.

Despite one doctor's firm prognosis of bipolar disorder, otherwise known as manic-depression, the staff ran with an initial diagnosis of schizophrenia. Lithium, the most effective drug used for bipolar disorder in the 1980's, had certain dangerous side effects that other drugs did not have. So, to ere on the side of caution, the hospital's medical majority ruled and they began to treat me with drugs that were typically used for schizophrenia.

That is when my ordeal only became worse. I have vague memories of ambling around in circles and squares with my arms mounted at my sides like some robot. I have other foggy memories of angry faces demanding that I take a shower. But I didn't know how to make the water warm; it was always cold. And *it hurt* to be in the cold water.

I was alone. There was nothing familiar in that place. Sterile, generic furniture—the same in every room. Strange faces, strange voices. I would crawl through a maze of confusion and anxious feelings all day, every day—unaware of space and time, stumbling around in concentric circles or rigid squares like some lab rat unable to find an exit to the winding hallways...or from my existence.

I remained in that disoriented state for some time until the private hospital was about to have me transported to a state hospital. But just before my scheduled transfer, the hospital staff finally acquiesced to the first doctor's insistence that they treat me with medications for bipolar disorder. Nothing else had worked, so they had no room to argue with him.

And voila—within ten days of being on that medication, I could, at least, *function* to some degree. I could shower myself and speak coherent sentences. A few more days later, and my old personality had mostly returned with the use of Lithium.

But treatment with Lithium had to be monitored closely in the initial trial. This required frequent blood tests to determine how much of the medication was in my bloodstream. The doctors had to make sure that this medication was at a therapeutic, but not *toxic* level.

Every morning from that point on, I would rouse to the jarring clicks of the door handle to my little room being opened. The dim light from the hallway, eclipsed by the nurse's figure, would soon spill onto my face as I laying squinting upward in effort to discern which staff member was on duty this time. I would then wake fully to the sound of rubber gloves snapping into position, and unknown fingers pressing into my arm to find a vein. I remember the shiny sight of their supply kits, which was about as comforting as the metal tray of tools that dentists must lay out before you. The instruments were a subtle reminder of who is going to be in charge for the next few minutes. Then would come their gentle preparation with the words, "This is going to stick a little." And in would go the needle, a tiny rod held firmly in soft tissue until the blood was drained. Then would come the cumbersome jolt as the nurse would replace the full vial with an empty one; sometimes a total of three vials were taken at one drawing. Upon discharge, my arms were blackened and bruised beyond belief. My veins had been torn so much that blood had spilled into my skin creating dark purple and blue blotches several inches above and below each elbow. But no matter—the word "discharge" was all I needed to know.

*Or so I thought.*

One last level, and no more to come for six months. Hallelujah. Since it was now "slim pickins" among the veins in my arms...the discharge nurse determined that taking blood from my hand was the only viable option.

So first came the cold, sterile stench of rubbing alcohol and the dreadful angst in my stomach as packages were being opened in a hurried rustle. Of course the experience would not be complete without the sinister glint of fluorescent lighting that flickered off the newly exposed needle tip. This would be a way of life from now on, like diabetes, they said—no point in complaining.

As I watched the tiny spearhead of the needle pierce the top of my young hand, it was in that moment of faint Christ-like imagery that I, oddly, felt most comforted. A strong, empowering notion bore down on my young soul: I BELONGED to Christ, I was safe with Him, I was here for His purpose, He would always be with me – even here, in this tiny small town lab room.

I was just a child, around 14 years old. All that really interested me was eating my fill of brownies and listening to Madonna. I was just one of a million other misfit Raggedy Anne and Andies who frequented that rehab unit, and a small and seemingly insignificant one at that. So these notions seemed extraneous, illogical.

*And what purpose could come from such a broken life?*

I had made my decision for Christ right before my parent's divorce the previous year after reading His Gospels, but still had very little knowledge of the Bible, and could only count on one hand the number of times that I'd been inside a church as a small child.

*So how could I, in my ignorance and eccentricities, be of worth or of use to anyone—much less to YAHWEH...the Supreme Being of the universe?*

I did not entertain those questions. They were good ones, but simply not strong enough to penetrate the warmth and joy I felt from this new sense of divine inclusion. Rich, red blood had filled the vial. The sample was complete. I flinched at the exiting needle, and smiled with my LORD. Little did I know, that such lives...are His specialty.

You see, in decades to come...I would suffer three more manic episodes that would, again, require hospitalization each time. And even to this day, I must manage this illness with medications through proper psychiatric care. Just as the Apostle Paul would always have the thorn in his flesh; this illness, it would not go away. But what I have found in Scripture, is that the Apostle was actually *blessed* to have his thorn. Clearly, the Christ told Paul, "...My grace is sufficient for you, for My strength is made perfect in weakness." (2nd Corinthians 12:9)

When we are stripped, and broken, laid bare by this world and its fallen state as manifested in our own human weakness and frailty...the less when can rely upon our*selves*. And the more we must cling to His grace, the closer to Him we become. I believe this is what led Paul to further proclaim in 2nd Corinthians 12:9-10, "Therefore most gladly I will rather boast in my infirmities, that the power of Christ may rest upon me. Therefore I take pleasure in infirmities, in reproaches, in needs, in persecutions, in distresses, for Christ's sake. For when I am weak, then I am strong."

Since that first manic episode, I have married and given birth to three wonderful children, one of whom has severe Autism, Intellectual Disabilities, and Diabetes. Through it all my husband and I have been married for over 29 years. And by God's grace I am able to carry on. But how is this all of this even possible after all that I have been through?

Clearly, the medications I take are *necessary* to ensure the stability of my moods, rest, and even sanity. I won't argue that.

However, they are NOT what (or *Who*) has...quite literally... *restored my soul.*

Truly, a person can be completely "sane" and simultaneously *miserable* – defeated, humiliated, and disgraced. But by the grace of God, I am none of those things anymore. Everyday, I have my challenges and my struggles as we all do...but there is a hope in me; there is JOY; there is life. And these attributes are not my own.

I know this because of times when I have drifted from the LORD, over the course of my life thus far...and I know the painful consequences of falling into that separation: angst, worry, arrogance, hatred for my fellow man over the slightest infraction, impatience, greed, covetousness, and the list of sins go on and on.

But when I take in the Gospel, and know that all these sins which separate me from the Holy God have been crucified with Christ in His perfect sacrifice for us on the cross...a joy feels me, a relief, a new found freedom stirs in me with the knowledge that nothing I can do or have done is of merit; that I don't have to "earn" my own salvation, that rather – it was *given* to me as a precious gift.

As it is written in John 3:16, "For God so loved the world, that He gave His only begotten Son, that whoever believes in Him shall not perish but have everlasting life."

It is then that I know where to credit this peace that surpasses all understanding! It is not derived from a trial-free life of ease and comfort. Nor is it to be credited to the local drug store, that much is for sure—and certainly not to my*self*.

But when I bow in daily repentance, in turning from my sins, to the Omnipotent, Almighty God...YAHWEH, the Ancient of Days...through CHRIST, He lifts me from my knees so that I can mount up on the wings of eagles. (Isaiah 40:31) He restores my soul. (Psalm 23:3) When my heart threatens to fail...He becomes the strength of my heart and my portion forever. (Psalm 73:26) And most importantly, I am reborn! (John 3:1-8)

This is because unyielding truth and amazing grace have been embodied together in a Living Man, Who is the Living GOD. His name is Jesus, the Christ. And only *He*...can set you *free*. (John 8:31-36)

# ACT OF GOD

When everywhere I look
there is nothing but defeat,
and when the scorch is blazing
from the desert's dying heat;

when skies withhold
the quench of rain
from thirsting plants, so tender;
when hope is like a barren field
held captive to its lender...

when every time
my eyes
descry
the mountains
I can't move,
when even faith is faint and weak
and God, I cannot prove...

the darkness closes in
but I will
*fear not*                                              *Isaiah 41:10
the night;
with dreams, deferred,
and pain, incurred,
I'll walk by faith, not sight.                    *2 Corinthians 5:7

For what's a desert without heat?
What are storms without the wind?
And what growth's sustained
or plants remain
without the rain
they send?

Truly, it was in a desert
where our LORD did pine for bread;
but chose to last
throughout his fast
on God's sweet Word, instead.                    *Matthew 4:1-4

Yes, it was in the storms
where our Savior chose to rest.
Knowing He would wake
for glory's sake
to calm the sea's dark, savage breast.           *Matthew 8:23-27

And it was on a bludgeoned cross—                    *Galatians 3:13
a scandal, shame, disgrace...                        *Hebrews 12:1-4
that Christ took up                    *Matthew 16:24-26, Luke 9:23
and drank the cup                                    *Matthew 26:39
of WRATH                                             *Isaiah 53:10
against our race...

of a people and our fallen state,            *Genesis, Chapter 3
the thrall of broken laws:                          *Isaiah 24:5
this yoke,              *Deuteronomy 28:48, Lamentations 1:14
he broke,
like light—He spoke
from darkness just because...

He saw that it was good                              *Genesis 1:4
to let Himself be known—                             *John 10:14-15
part night from day                                  *Genesis 1:5
and make a Way                                       *John 14:6
for our inward, wordless groans.                     *Romans 8:26-27

Let them cry out,
let earth give shout!                                *Psalm 66:4

Through famine, quake, and fire…
that seasons bring
for death's no sting                                    *1 Corinthians 15:55
or souls it can acquire…

if even in our suffering,
we have repented, rejoiced, and reveled:               *Romans 5:1-5
knowing in the flood
of God's Own blood—
our debt of sin's been leveled!                        *Colossians 2:13-14

# ALL THAT YOU ARE

Help me, LORD,
when
I am
weak.
Let me find You
when I seek.                                    *Matthew 7:7-8

For
I am
straying
as of late;
my burdens, heavy—
my heart, it hates…

so prone to drift,
like so much *wood*;                            *Deuteronomy 4:28
so much temptation,
I've not withstood.

I am
a branch                                        *John 15:6
that's withering, cracked;
fit to be burned,
for virtues, lacked.

So dry, I thirst.
I hunger, crave                                 *Matthew 5:6
for founts of grace—
that You might save…

me from these times
when I don't feel it;
when truth is drown
and lies conceal it.

When all that's in me
is of this world;                                    *1 John 2:16
when
I am
snatched and whisked and swirled...

into a cyclone, funneled away—
by winds
unknown,                                            *Ephesians 4:14
untamed,
and scathed.

So far from home,
no yellow brick
layed out before
my steps, so quick...

to head in any ole direction;
thrown by the sea's                                *James 1:6
stern, cold rejection...

to an abyss
where Nothing reigns
but malice, scorn, and bitter pains...

that leave my spirit
deaf and dumb,
that kill within—
nervose, but numb.

Apart from You,
this is all;
this chasm spawned
with Adam's fall.                                   *Genesis, Chapter 3

But from that fall,
we rise again—
through You,                                        *1ˢᵗ Corinthians 15:21-22

so great,
Who trampled sin...

and made our debt void and erased,                    *Colossians 2:13-14
Who took upon Yourself disgrace.

So that when I'm faint
from hungering strife—
**You Are**,
from Heav'n, my *Bread of Life*.                         *John 6:35

And when I'm in darkness,
tossed and twirled,
**You Are**
the calm *Light of the World*.                           *John 8:12

When none I recognize or know...
**You Are**
the *Door* through Whom I go.                            *John 10:7-9

When hirelings flea,
wolves scatter sheep...
**You Are**
the *Shepherd, Good*,                                    *John 10:11, 14
His flock to keep.

When death has cut us like a knife,
**You Are**
the *Resurrection and the Life*.                         *John 11:25

When I am lost, lied to, in strife...
**You Are**
*the Way, the Truth, the Life*.                          *John 14:6

And when I'm that dying branch or root,
**You Are**
the *Vine* bearing in me, fruit.                         *John 15:1

# AN ANSWER TO HIS CHILD

I've run from God and hid my face                    *Isaiah 53:3
in sin, despair, and deep disgrace...

into a corner, dark and cold,
as night rolls in and darkness told...

me all the reasons for my shame
that I am lost, no one to blame.

And yet a tender whisper calls                       *1 Kings 19:12
from deep within my prison walls...

My Advocate                                          *1 John 2:1
Physician, Great...                                  *Luke 5:31-31
My Shepherd, Good                                    *John 10:11-15
and Sacred Gate...                                   *John 10:9

He knows I
*hunger*
He knows I
*thirst*                                             *Matthew 5:6
He knows I'm a
child of Adam, cursed.                    *Genesis 3:16-19, Romans 5:19

But I know this now,
my case He'll plead.
And I know He is all
I'll ever need.                                      *2 Peter 1:3

The Bread of Life                                    *John 6:35
and water, living...                         *John 4:7-30 sufficient
grace--                                      *2nd Corinthians 12:9
my sin, forgiving ...                                *1 John 1:9

It is for us
He came to die,                                          *John 3:16
and hunger – thirst,
He satisfies...                                          *Psalm 107:9

He calls to us, "...follow Me..."                        *Matthew 16:24
from virgin womb                        *Isaiah 7:14, Matthew 1:18-25
and hallowed tree                                 *Galatians 3:13-14

to die to self and turn from sin
and rise with Him, new again...                          *Romans 6:8

straight to that dark and desperate day
when He returns and has His Way...

when the world is filled with Godly sorrow
once and for all, this yet, tomorrow...

when skies turn to sackcloth, black                      *Revelation 6:12
with the moon as blood - He's coming back                *Revelation 22:20

for all that's His, for everything,                      *Psalm 50:10-12
He spoke to life 'mid seraph wings                       *Genesis 1

with eyes aflame that search for us,                     *Revelation 19:12
His virgin bride,                                   *2 Corinthians 11:2
Him we can trust.

# AUDIENCE OF ONE

For whom is art?
For whom, its worth?
For whom's Creation?                    *1 Chronicles 29:11, Colossians1:16
...*or soul's rebirth?*                                    *John 3:1-15

For who do we write, sculpt, or paint?
For who do we sing or act or faint?
For what is our purpose - crass or quaint?
What was the will
in feathered quills
of saints?

To each his own, an audience of sorts,
except to me...but One, whose courts,
I'll enter in with thanks and praise                    *Psalm 100:4
and lift a joyful noise with spirits raised.            *Psalm 100:1

I have no book signings.
There's no grandeur to my game.
And Hollywood will not celebrate
my faith on walks of fame.

No one wants my autograph.
No one caters to my whim.
But all of this is fine with me,
because it's not about me – but Him.

I have no adoring fans,
no coveted Rolls Royce.
I have no crowds to follow me
and yet I still rejoice.

I have no invitations,
no chance to go and speak.

I've no real hope of exposure,
only to find what I do seek.                        *Matthew 7:7

I've no riches, stocks, or bonds.
I've no Bentley, furs, or fame.
I've no real estate.
It's not my fate...
but a mansion in His name.                          *John 14:2

No one takes my photograph.
No one flatters my every choice.
No one builds for me a sound system,
and yet I have a voice.

And I will lift it now,
I'll wield it like a sword;                          *Ephesians 6:17
not as to break a tender reed,                       *Isaiah 42:3
but to honor my dear LORD.

He sees a sparrow as it falls.                       *Matthew 10:29
He's numbered the hairs on my head.                  *Matthew 10:30
Then can He
not see
my agony
in every line, not read?

Can he not know
depths of my soul,
can't I trust Him with my heart?
Its sickened deceit,                                 *Jeremiah 17:9
ultimate defeat,
and hope it, He'll set apart?

Wrestle with it,
LORD of mine –                                       *Genesis 32:24-28
that Your Word not be misused...

whether vain,
or proud refrain,
by my melody and muse.

For I've no microphone
to reach the throne,
nothing but hope and prayer...
that He'll turn a stone                    *Ezekiel 36:26; Matthew 3:9
into His own,
and on that I cast my care.                              *1 Peter 5:7

For what profits me
to gain the world
if my soul's lost from God, His Son?              *Mark 8:36
He's the only Way                                          *John 14:6
to whom I play,
my sweet Audience of One.

# BE STILL AND KNOW

Be still and know                                    *Psalm 46:10
that
God is
there,
in all moments
fully aware.                              *Psalm 147:5, Isaiah 40:28

Be still and know
that
God is
He, Who died for you                               *1 Peter2:21-25
on Calvary's Tree.                                 *Galatians 3:13

Be still and know
for just this reason,
that
God is
with you                                           *Matthew 28:20
through all seasons.                            *Ecclesiastes 3:1-8

Be still and know
God rules the graves...     *1st Corinthians 15:24-26, Revelation 1:18
they do not keep
the ones Christ saves!

Be still and know
that
God is
near,                                                *James 4:8
'spite all your angst
and nervous fear.

Be still and know
God is
the Way,

the Truth, and Life
and that He stays...

deep within your
conscious soul,
your groaning cries
that take a role...

above Him
~in your heart~
some, now and then--
yet He'll forgive
this present sin...

that separates you
to His grief;
for He can offer
sweet relief…

from all your pain
and heartache so,
it is important
that you know...

His passion for you, Bride,
is new--
and His commitment
tried and true!

He sees that all His sheep are fed,
not left to starve or even dread...

but cast their cares
on Him instead,
as every page
they've turned and read...

*John 14:6

*1 Corinthians 3:16
*Romans 8:26

*Ephesians 5:32, Revelation 19:7

*John 21:17

*Psalm 55:22, 1 Peter 5:7

of His bold words
and pious claims--
so rest assured
God is
the same.

*Matthew 24:35

*Hebrews 13:8

Look now to His
strong staff and rod.
Be still and know
that He is God.

*Psalm 23:4

# BE YE HOLY

Set apart,                                              *Jeremiah 1:5
He has you called by name…                              *Isaiah 43:1
no more
grieving, endless shame.                                *Revelation 21:4

Set apart,
He has made you whole…                                  *Mark 5:34
no more
straying from the fold.                                 *Luke 15:1-7

Set apart,                                              *1 Peter 5:13-15
He has brought you to life…                             *Romans 6:4
no more
fear of death and strife.        *1 Corinthians 15:55, 2 Timothy 1:10

Consecrated,
once and for all
by His choice                                           *Ephesians 1:4
'spite Adam's fall.                             *Genesis, Chapter 3

Consecrated,
you have been
given victory                                   *1 Corinthians 15:57
over sin.

Consecrated,
you are made pure                                       *Isaiah 1:18
by the wounds
He did endure.                             *Isaiah 53:5, 1 Peter 2:24

HOLY
no wrinkle, spot, or blemish...
we'll base eternity
on this premise:

God loves the world so,
that angels sing...
about the ransom
of our King!

*1 Peter 1:16
*Ephesians 5:27


*John 3:16
*Luke 2:13-14
*Matthew 20:28, Luke 10:45
*John 18:37, Revelation 19:16

# BRUSH STROKES

a canvas, clean
a Way made plain                                    *John 14:6
'spite all my paint
and sin and stain

it's so pristine
so white, so pure
and cannot tempt                                    *James 1:13
us or allure

for it is perfect
undefiled,
and
set apart
for tempers mild

who will not trash it
at the sight
of a mistake
or coming plight

who will in modest
temperance be
content to turn                                     *Acts 3:19
the brush and see                              *Matthew 13:16

what majesty will be created
for those who've sought
and pined
and waited                                          *Isaiah 40:31

for strength renewed
an eagle's wing
a walk not faint
in death, no sting                          *1 Corinthians 15:55

and yet it's easy
understand
to question movements
by the hand

of the Artist's sudden plan
or so it seems
as we withstand

the disappearing grand designs
of our own thoughts and wants and minds          *Job 17:11

until we near the brink of sanity
until we see that all is vanity          *Ecclesiastes 1:2

and then surrender          *Mark 8:35
to the sight
of His perspective,          *Isaiah 55:9
hue, and Light...          *John 8:12

as these transform a lowly page
to new creation's          *2nd Corinthians 5:17
war that's waged

'gainst principalities and powers          *Ephesians 6:12-13
in every age
and passing hour

that we keep watch          *Mark 13:35
and linger much
to see
the Artist's graceful touch          *Matthew 20:33-34

from which His fingertips does flow
an eloquence in painful throes

like Mother Moses in the reeds          *Exodus 2:3
we sense a primal aching need

to see our own, from chains, now freed
as passion grows and colors bleed

poured out                                              *Matthew 26:28
as offering to all
to ears that hear                                       *Matthew 13:16
there comes a call                                      *Romans 11:29

to see this stoic Master peace                          *Isaiah 9:6
come back to life                              *1 Corinthians 15:20-27
and never cease

His work in progress as it stands                    *Philippians 1:6
in stars of skies and grains of sand...                *Genesis 22:17

are burdens light and easy yokes                   *Matthew 11:28-30
from His divine and guiding strokes.

# BY MOTHER'S GRAVE

For Pat Todd, My Late Mother-in-Law

Loss and grief,
fear and strife...
money spent
and my life

Is out of dreams,
ambition dies
as night crawls round
and family ties

are in the ground
no more to be
a sheltering voice
that comforts me...

reminding of a childhood home
where cares were few
no need to roam

But now I'm grown
and you are gone
as memories fade
within the dawn...

of a new day with troubles new,
problems to solve and things to do.

But like a dream upon the wake,
your essence comes just for my sake—

surrounding me and all my senses!
The scent of you strips my defenses,

and leaves me bare, bereft, undone.
Nowhere to hide, no way to run.

And if I could, why would I leave?
If this all I've left to grieve?

A glimpse of you, a shadow past
returns to me and at long last.

Your whisper rough, but faint I feel
and pine for times when it seems real.

You acted well, your role as sage
if all the world is just a stage...

playing your Naomi to my Ruth,                    *Ruth 1:1-18
I clung to you, sayer of sooth...

who told me that our God is good—
that faith to keep, of this I should.

And that I did, your God is mine!
So I will see you again sometime...

when you are new and whole again,
apart from death and pain and grievous sin.

Though our vile bodies, all will perish,
and leave only cold stones to cherish—

we will be raised, restored, equipped
Into our heavenly citizenship!                    *Philippians 3:20-21

Where cancer can no longer thrive—
where we are with the Christ, *alive!*

So when He comes with outstretched hand,
I know just where I want to stand...

at the first sight of One Who Saves,
I want to be...by Mother's grave.

Author's Note:

Like so many daughters-in-laws...I spent the first decade or so grumbling about my mother-in-law's choice words and turns of phrase that I chose to take personally. But with my fourth manic episode, wherein I had to be placed – again – in a hospital, I turned to her in tears...begging for a place to stay should, in my illness-induced paranoia, something happen to our family. She took my hands in her, and promised me that I would always have a home with her. So much wasted time. In the last five years of her life, I began to cherish her as a mom. I finally loved her. And then, she was gone. So, don't waste time, because it is not promised. Make amends and love deeply, as soon as you can, for the time that you are given.

# CAST OF FINAL CARES

A Hospice Poem

Some say they see faint rays of light,          *John 8:12
the sudden flashing pass...
of the Comforter                          *John 16:7
who's welcoming
the ones going at last.

Some say they see the darkened move
of shadows here and there.
And some are 'fraid,
as these delay,
and stop to tarry where...

we rush and run
under the sun
and moon
as it falls night,
we scramble 'gainst the morn,
with all muscle and might...

for another life that's lost
'mid our angst and wrath,
but should we
from bended knee
question the Savior's path?

These rays of light comes beckoning,
to take the chosen Home,
as shadows cloaked in mystery
down quiet halls do roam...

into the night
during our fright
to find a open Gate,                      *John 10:9
and a wedding feast         *Revelation 19:7-8

for the least
of these...                                         *Matthew 25:40-45
where Bridegroom waits.                              *Revelation 19:7

And so there is no thing to fear,
no dreaded evil there—
only the LORD,
Whose grace affords,
souls casting final cares.                           *1 Peter 5:6-7

Author's Note:
When I served as a Certified Nursing Aide in hospice care, I sometimes would hear nurses talk of what they believe to be supernatural forces at work. They had seen certain flashes of light and shadows on occasion from the corners of their eyes while caring for terminally ill patients. These sightings do not occur every time someone dies. However, when they are seen...you can bet, someone has passed, or will pass, on that very same shift. One LVN asked her pastor what the shadows might be. She feared that they might be some dark and evil presence. But her pastor said that in his opinion, no. He suggested that the shadows might simply be the souls of those departed...who are walking in search of the Light of the World, Jesus Christ, who has come to take them Home.

# CHRIST IS

Where are You, God?
In my aches and pain,
the constant groaning,                    *Romans 8:26-27
driving me insane.

Where are You, God?
When I'm alone...
can You hear me
from Your throne?

Where are You, God?
In my loss and fear...
I draw close to You,
but are You near?                          *James 4:8

Though these questions
cut like a knife—
through all the pain,
and grief, and strife...

that cripple me
in fervent rage,
a compelling Presence
leaps off the page:

Christ is
your present Friend,                       *John 15:15
your God, your Father
til the end.

Christ is the wind                         *John 3:8
that comforts you.                         *John 14:16
Christ is the sweet
fresh fallen dew.                      *Deuteronomy 32:2

Christ is the dawn
of a new day,
where mercy's new                                    *Lamentations 3:22-24
and fear's at bay.

Christ is the Waker                                        *Revelation 3:2
and the Keep                                               *Psalm 121:5
of those you love
who've gone asleep!                              *1 Corinthians 15:51

Christ is the spring
in bloom for you,                                          *Hosea 6:3
Christ is the change
that makes you new.                                  *Revelation 21:5

Christ is the rich
redeeming blood,                                      *Ephesians 1:7-10
Christ is the fast
swift-coming flood!           *Matthew 24:36-39; Luke 17:26-27

Christ is the song              *Psalm 118:14; Isaiah 12:2
that makes you sing.
Christ is your Groom,                               *Ephesians 5:22-33
you have His ring.

Christ is the first,
Christ is the last                                      *Revelation 22:13
onto Whom
your cares now cast!                                    *1 Peter 5:7

Christ the One
upon the cross.
Christ is my *hope*...                                   *1 Peter 1:3-5
when hope seems lost.

# CHRISTMAS POEM

A Baby breathed into a womb,
a girl so young and frail...                           *Luke 1:26-38
a journey of some distance
where Simeon would foretell                             *Luke 2:21-35

the sweet redemption
that this Child
would bring to Israel
amid all Anna's praises                                 *Luke 2:36-38
with thanks to God, as well...

the God Who stirred His life inside,                    *Luke 1:26-35
the God Who bore our nails...                      *Colossians 2:13-14
the God Who comes to ravage us,
like fierce and unseen gales                              *John 3:8
the God Who calms the seas,                            *Mark 4:35-41
and throws a prophet in the whale.                      *Jonah 1:17

He also came as gentle Child,
a Child without a home
in this dark world
to virgin girl—
humble manger, as His throne.                             *Luke 2:7

Who is this Child...?
What is this Truth...?                                    *John 14:6
That we must come to embrace...?
What stoic glory
from this story
now stares us in the face...?

It's that for all His love                               *John 3:16
poured out for the human race,
there was no room                                         *Luke 2:7

and a borrowed tomb                                   *Luke 23:50-54
is where we finally had Him placed.

Look flat into the fact of that,
glare straight into its shame,
and know that we're the ones
He still gives the right
to call His name!                                     *Hebrews 4:16

Let dead ones quicken
as we are stricken
by a sword                                            *Hebrews 4:12
that pierces through...
our mind and marrow
on the way, so narrow,                                *Matthew 7:14
as creatures who are renewed.                *2nd Corinthians 5:17

Like that this Baby came
into a world so cold,
and still this Baby comes
into desperate, wayward souls:

to coo just as a precious Dove
would call a tender mate...
to redeem humanity
in all her fallen state;
to call her blessed,
should she confess,
and fall prostrate 'fore His gates;

to absolve His people
of their sin—without a trace...
this God Who wills
that we be still,                                     *Psalm 46:10
and be humbled                                        *Matthew 23:12
by His grace!

# CINDERELLA'S HOUR

raw and white-gray
are the ashes today as
smoke is blown
from faces nearby,
as pass time is made of
flicking cinders
at death's door
while
white water falls
down from
the heartland, beating still—
holding its breath
and beholding beauty,
in awe of
witch-ever's work
will bring them prosperity
each hour psychic's
nickel & dime
the desperate to death,
all seeking only
       that sixth grammy
       that sixth sweet sugar pill
       that sixth stolen ego, bought & sold
but none for me, see
I spend my day
keeping doctors at bay
with their sufficient bedside manner
as the nurses hover
while their hair—whether
       black, brown, red, gold, or white
eclipses a distant hall light,
creating halos
that shine brightly
about their
bobby pins and butterfly clips,

as compassionate eyes
search for
an outstretched vein
in vain
to fill a vial, vile
deed that's been done—
        been transferred,
        out of home,
        been alienated,
        bought & sold,
        like so many acres,
        like distant generations, and...
...I watch the needle
steal my blood—a stick, a prick
and off to the left,
the east,
where the wicked live
I see that
money has changed hands
again, changed two faces
into one
behind a podium,
promising 2$^{nd}$ sight—
words stirred by silver spoons
and silver tongues
are stained by them...
civil shovels
bury the truth
leaving only their
lucrative make-believe
sickening music pipes
on and around we go on
wooden horses
up and down...
...as blood is found,
spurting in and filling up—
then the needle's taken out
by miscellaneous hands

in the early morning
and miscellaneous faces
by flashlights in the night—
all bearing gentle, gentile smiles
and sympathetic eyes
unlike
the snake eyes
of the great pretenders...
and me,
a lowly leper
who cannot change her spots,
in need of a healing touch
to make me whole again,                              *Mark 5:34
afforded barely
through
God's *salt*                                          *Matthew 5:13
of the earth.

Author's Note:
In 1996, I was hospitalized for the third time in my life with a manic
episode. I had stayed off Lithium with the birth of our second child
for too long. Politics, and my obsessions with them, only added to
my confusion and angst. It in that year that the controversial partial-
birth abortion became legal with a presidential veto. It seemed to me
that our nation had put infants on the alter for sacrifice. I had lost
hope in our leaders. I had lost hope in my own sanity, yet again, with
the slings and arrows of bipolar disorder. So these broken thoughts,
strung together in failing lucidity, came to me and some time after
my release I penned them into this poem to convey my suffering;
but moreover, to praise the only hope that never failed me who was
Jesus Christ, my LORD.

# CLOTHED WITH CHRIST

Doldrums loom
and I'm a waste
as barren land,
like acid, tastes...

the bitter pill
I have to swallow,
the pity pit
in which I wallow.

I do not feel Your love for people,
even as I stand beneath Your steeple.

Your Word is distant to my heart.
And I am weak, so torn apart.

Drifting now toward sleep,                    *1st Thessalonians 5:6
and naked—                                     *Revelation 15:16
stripped so bare;
come get Your clay                             *Jeremiah 18:1-11
and have Your Way                                   *Acts 24:14
'fore sin's got me in its snare.

LORD, pick me up,
and throw me down...
send me crashing on the ground.

Scatter me,                                    *Acts 8:1,4; 11:19
and spread my parts
til
I AM                                           *Exodus 3:14
satisfied...
break in me the spirit, wicked,
until
I am
truly tried.

Set me in the fire;                                          *Jeremiah 23:29
hold me Your vice...
melt, in me, impurities                                      *Malachi 3:2-4
and cut me with Your knife.                                  *Hebrews 4:12

Your blade as sharp as iron,                                 *Proverbs 27:17
Your Word as hard as Truth—                                  *John 14:6
and send me 'fore the lions;                                 *Daniel, Chapter 6
let me seem to some, uncouth...

lacking in sophistication,
social norms,
and all that's polished:
let me reside
in You, abide,                                               *John 15:4
till lies are all demolished!

Break in me the ego,
the vanity of pride...                   *Proverbs 16:18, Ecclesiastes 2:11
strip me of many vices
for from You, sin cannot hide.

You know this wretched heart of mine,
You see it's sickened state...                               *Jeremiah 17:9
You call me to Your Word
that I might examine                                  *2nd Corinthians 13:5
my grim fate--

apart from You,
a branch that withers;                                       *John 15:5
fit only for the fire...                                     *Revelation 20:10
cut off as the wicked,                                       *Psalm 37:28
subject to Your wrath and ire.

There is a loss I fear
even more than Hell's contempt
and that is this
strange, dark abyss                                          *Revelation 20:3

where I cannot attempt...
to call Your name
for in my shame
the enemy has emptied

me of the Good News                                     \*1 Corinthians 15:1-2
that You have done it all;                                  \*1 John 2:2
that I was never
righteous enough
to answer any call.

But now I'll lift my eyes                                     \*Psalm 121:1
up to Heaven's grace,                                  \*Hebrews 4:16
with faith as my strong shield;                            \*Ephesians 6:16
and find Your joy                                    \*John 15:11
like treasure
that's been hidden in a field!                          \*Matthew 13:44

I'll take up Your spirit's sword;                        \*Ephesians 6:17
and with it I will wield
all my armor                                     \*Ephesians 6:11
as a faithful farmer                               \*Matthew 13:3-8
whose seeds have grown to yield...

good fruit,                                     \*Matthew:7:18
      a harvest                           \*2nd Corinthians 9:10
           in our age
wearing truth's own belt                             \*Ephesians 6:14
in prayer, I've knelt
working for the promised wage.                 \*Matthew 20:1-16

Then I'll don my helmet,                           \*Ephesians 6:17
salvation's headstrong quest;
with the plate of righteousness                \*Ephesians 6:14
kept upright and abreast.

Avoiding arrows—                                    *Ephesians 6:16
their fiery powers;
with news of peace, I'll shod                       *Ephesians 6:15
these feet, washed clean,                            *John 13:1-17
by my true King                                      *John 18:37
all by the grace of God.                            *Ephesians 4:7

# CORD OF THREE

In good times & bad,
a marriage still will stand;
when God be at the head
of all the couple's plans.

Because the day is long,
& the journey
can take its tolls;
but won't when
He is rooted deeply
in the couple's souls.

Yes, that is truly when
two flesh have
become one...                                    *Genesis 2:24
for now they dock
up on the Rock                                   *Matthew 7:24-27
through storms calmed                            *Luke 8:22-25
by God's own Son.

And should their joy
be stolen; their hearts
be made to faint,
as loved ones fly
~Sweet By & By~
they have perseverance
of the saints!

Because, you see,
it is written!
Three strands make
a stronger cord,                                 *Ecclesiastes 4:12
when knots are tied
& sanctified
in Jesus Christ, our LORD!                       *Mark 10:9

# CUSHIONED PEWS

I sit on top the cushioned pews
with thoughts that race and wander.
I made it here
on time, for once,
'spite hours that I've squandered.

I try to focus,
sing the songs,
or make a joyful noise.                                        *Psalm 98:4
I nod or grin,
confess my sin,                                                *James 5:16
like good girls and boys.

I listen to the preacher.
          *But do I…*
ever HEAR?                                              *Matthew 13:15
          Or do I SEE                                   *Matthew 13:15
the Truth                                                      *John 14:6
that he
expounds as I watch and leer?

For inside
there's something
nagging me –
a panting, aching need                                        *Psalm 42:1
to know more than
these rituals can
ever dare to calm                          *Matthew 8:26, Mark 4:39
or feed.                                                       *John 6:27

What do I lack
on cushioned pews…?
Their pattern I helped to pick
at one of countless meetings
and soul-defeating
assurances my heart's not sick.                           *Jeremiah 17:9

For yes, indeed,
I have it all...
a big house on the hill;
an education,
stocks and bonds –
so why
an emptiness I can't fill?                    *Proverbs 27:29, Ecclesiastes 1

That brooding, deep reminder...
that moment
when no one sees
me crying in the shower,
successes crumbling
at my knees.

Because, you see,
I'm *LOST* inside –
craving what I've never known,
and cold tradition
or choral rendition
cannot sooth like wordless groans...                    *Romans 8:26

that intercede
for this unbruised reed,                    *Isaiah 42:3
offered on my behalf
where in Heaven
(seventy times seven)                    *Matthew 18:21-22
Father slays the fatted calf!                    *Luke 15:23

So many years
bring me to tears                    *2nd Corinthians 7:9-10
all of which I was a liar...
to God, self, and man.
Who'll understand?
Or am I preaching to the choir?

Once lost                                          *Luke 15:24
between the cushioned pews
like a coin                                      *Luke 15:8-10
of precious worth…
now found                                          *Luke 15:24
by faithful,                              *2<sup>nd</sup> Timothy 2:13
blood-stained palms,                             *Isaiah 49:16
who've delivered                                  *Psalm 34:17
*my new birth!*                                      *John 3:5

# DARKEST BEFORE THE DAWN

Street lights shine
through mini-blinds,
lighting my little room—leaving
horizontal shadow lines
against the head board.
They are comforting—remind me
life goes on
outside my four walls at night;
and these lights
shield us from
the feared darkness
that would only be
the moonlight
coming clean
as eschewed sunlight from
yesterday. Back when
we could breathe
fresh air
...when doors were left unlocked
(as Grandma claimed)
and
boys and girls
could play outside
(without drive-bys)
pr pedophiles
who would
        slip through
the unforeseen cracks in
lady liberty
that now rip her
bell
up the middle
and all apart.
But back then
were also

jim crow laws
and
crosses
getting burned.
Yes, history teaches
(but do we learn)
from other dark thoughts
and consequences:
      swastikas symbolizing
      unbridled hate which fed on
      His Chosen Ones           *Deuteronomy 7:6
      like hungry fires-burning
      and churning, ravenous,
      unending, insatiable, incessant
      appetites           *1 Peter 5:8
      that sought out
      imagined enemies everywhere—a hatred
that will eventually
feed on itself someday,
will choke on
its own
rough ferocity.

So now…
where's our preverbial
Road Not Taken
to lead us
back to Virtue…
but was there ever virtue…?
If we could betray, deny, and crucify     *Matthew 27:32-56
our only Hope?     *Isaiah 42:1-4, Matthew 12:15-21

Isn't there a safe place
where Light is brighter     *Revelation 21:23
than our electric man-made lamps
cluttered along our little roads
and a Light     *John 8:12
brighter still

than the
second rate sunshine
off our moon...
where there
are straight and narrowed...                        *Matthew 7:14
where
Adonai
is one with us and                              *1 Corinthians 13:12
His Bright Son                        *1 John 4:14-15, Revelation 22:5
will radiate
        to light
            the Way                                    *John 14:6
and warm our souls?

A Place...                                           *John 14:2-4
where darkness simply is not,
and so need not,
be feared.

# DEAR GOD

Dear God,
I know that You are there.
I know You take the time to care.

I know You see me in my state
of darkened dreams, ambition's fate...

I know You well enough to hear                    *Matthew 13:16
Your guiding voice, so crystal clear:                  *John 10:27

You chase me when I've run too far.
You light my path,                                  *Psalm 119:105
Bright Morning Star!                            *Revelation 22:16

You give me grace when I deserve
hellfire instead, and so I've learned...

to walk a narrow, holy Way,                         *Matthew 7:14
'fore Your impending Judgment Day,

that comes to all despite belief
...*or lack thereof;*
so let me keep

all Your commands,
loving you as LORD
for all the joy Heaven affords.

For I starve when doubt
plagues like a drought,
as I suffer from life's pain;
but delight in You,
my God most true,
like a rose who craves the rain!

And this is what You long to hear,
from souls to whom You will draw near...                    *James 4:8

and calm the raging, stormy fears
of hell itself, of death, and tears.

But God,
what can I give to You...
Who made earth, moon, and sun?                              *Psalm 33:6-9
Dear God,
what offering might please
from my sickened heart, undone?                             *Jeremiah 17:9

For You count the atoms – orchestrate
the ocean's depth and vast of space!                        *Genesis 1:20

So break my heart and make it new,            *Revelation 21:5
like a King's palatial quarters...
that's been redone
fit for Your Son
beyond mere brick and mortar.

And let Him come and reign in it.
I'll suffer the cost, but remain in it!

Dear God,
do finish what You've begun...                              *Philippians 1:6
for what wants have You, Almighty One?
'Cept for the glory of Your Son,
revealed in faith that He has won!

# DEEPER THINGS

Worn hymnals and an alter call;
the belfry, lantern, spire...
and
I AM                                 *Exodus 3:14, Mark 14:62
there...
where whispered prayers
cast all our cares                            *1 Peter 5:7
of those who dare
confront our
worst desires.

But not so most would notice,
and not so most would see;               *Matthew 13:13-15
with sickened heart                        *Jeremiah 17:9
I play the part
bowing on my knees...

and stand when I'm to stand;
and pray when I'm to pray.
I sing when I'm to sing;
And say what I should say.

The Bible sits behind my pew
commanding to obey:
as I squirm,
a lowly worm,                              *Psalm 22:6
who dreads its Judgment Day...        *Joel 2:31, Acts 2:20

for I follow like a sheep                      *John 10:4
until I want my way,
then stumble—fall;                       *John 11:10
avoid God's call,
and quickly go astray.                     *Isaiah 53:6

But not so most would notice,
and not out in the Light;                                    *John 8:12
for darkness brings                            *Matthew 6:23, John 3:19
these deeper things
that are hidden out of sight...

where I alone can see them
and I know they are there
haunting me
and taunting me
like a beast caught in a snare—              *Eccl 9:12, 1 Thess 5:1-4

by deeper things
only the King                                        *Revelation 19:16
could know lurk in my mind;
things that feed
on souls and breed—things
only the King                                            *Mark 9:14-29
can bind.

For all will be made public                               *Luke 8:17
and all will be revealed,
when from the Throne                               *Revelation 4:1-6
the One Who's known                                       *John 10:14
will open seven seals.                               *Revelation 5:5

So I'll dig up these
these deeper things,
their corpse I tried to hide;
and confess
my nasty mess
to all whom I have lied.

So that many notice
and so that many see:                              *Matthew 13:16
Christ is LORD                                   *2 Corinthians 4:5
Whose grace affords
a hallowed, scarlet tree...                          *Galatians 3:13

to which, I cling;
nail deeper things                                         *Colossians 2:13-14
with their failed façade;
then soar on wings,                                          *Isaiah 40:31
holy apron strings,
trusting in no thing—
but God.                                                      *Psalm 9:10

# DRAW NEAR TO GOD

God, where am I in my grief?
Apart from You, there's no relief.

Just a waiting, open grave
is sin that lures me like its slave...

so that I fall, but seldom kneel,
my life it takes – my joy, it steals...                    *John 10:10

until the moment that I face
the fact I cannot run this race,                          *Hebrews 12:1

and cast my cares on You instead                          *1 Peter 5:7
Who walked the seas                                *Matthew 14:22-27
and raised the dead...                                 *John 11:38-43

Who calms a raging storm in me
by grace, through faith, that I believe.              *Ephesians 2:8-9

To pain, You are the healing Balm.                    *Jeremiah 8:22
To sleep, You are the waking Psalm.                        *Psalm 3:5

To doubt, You are the faith, by far;
To night, the Bright and Morning Star.              *Revelation 22:16

To hunger, You're the bread, to feed;                      *John 6:35
To thirst, the fountain we all need.          *Isaiah 55:1, John 4:5-14

that breaks through all our stony hearts              *Ezekiel 36:26
that crushes fear and sets apart

this soul as I draw near to You,
draw near to me – Your word, that's true.                 *James 4:8

# EMPTY TOMB

What power comes from
an empty tomb...?
What joy is in a grave...?
Where we have left
the very ones we hoped our God would save...?
And why should we sing
that death's no sting                    *1 Corinthians 15:55-57
while we hide like Elijah in the cave...?          *1 Kings 19:1-17

For we're hard as stone,
and dead
in trespass deep.
We are that wayward son,                    *Luke 15:11-32
that ever-roaming sheep.        *Matthew 18:12-14, Luke 15:3-7

And we can't forgive
when angers rise,
like rain withheld
by brooding skies.

Our dreams dry up
like streams in drought,
and faith is weak
for we're in doubt.

Hard envy smolders
cremating peace—
our soul's a seething wraith.
And we covet all
as bitter Saul                    *1 Samuel, Chapters 18-19
apart from David's faith.

For every time
we vie
to try

and turn a brand new leaf,
our grotesque failures
snare us
under chains of looming grief.

And we are spent,
just all used up,
clay vessels
void of hope—
with ego bruised
now life, we rue,
left wondering how to cope.

We cannot salvage all the shards
that once had housed our passion
and stitch them back together
in some vain and clumsy fashion.

We can't pour from an unwashed cup.       *Matthew 23:25-26
We cannot right this wrong.
We're only weak
and can only seek       *Matthew 7:7-8
Jesus Christ, who makes us strong.    *Isaiah 40:29, 1 Peter 5:10

He calls the lowly fisherman,    *Matthew 4:18-22, Luke 5:1-11
absolves the sinful harlot.       *John 8:3-11
He mends the broken part of us,
redeeming all our sins, so scarlet.

He parts the sea.       *Exodus 14:15- 21
He wakes the dead.    *Mark 5:35-43, John 11:43-44
He narrows the path       *Matthew 7:14
On which we're led.

He chastens us in sweet rebuke
that saves our souls of ill repute.

He calms the sea,
quiets the storm,     *Matthew 8:23-27, Mark 4:35-41, Luke 8: 22-25
raging in the flesh
from which we're formed.

He cradles our infant spirits
made new
at each rebirth,                                        *John 3:1-3
so much
we see                                                 *Matthew 13:16
how we are free...
and how much He is worth.

So crown Him with many crowns.              *Revelation 19:11-18
wash His feet
in fine perfume.              *Matthew 26:6-13, Luke 7:36-50
For He quenches thirst                              *Matthew 5:6
with living water                          *John 4:13-14; 7:37-38
poured from
an empty tomb.        *Matthew 28; Mark 16; Luke 24; John 20

# FAITH HAS MADE YOU

When everything is lost and wrong...
when night is dark and day is long...

my soul screams out from constant pain
I call to You throughout the strain ...

and it is You Who gives me rest,                    *Matthew 11:29
not those who claim to know God's best,

for in Your Word, you said there'd be
this suffering and desperate pleas                  *Matthew 10:16

to know You more each passing day,
to chase You down like jars of clay              *2 Corinthians 4:7-9

who need the Potter's steady hand                    *Jeremiah 18:4
-like stars at night, like grains of sand-        *Genesis 22:17-18

so numerous and yet diverse...
set us apart, and break a curse;                    *Exodus 20:4-6

so that in all we do or claim,                   *Colossians 3:23-24
we glorify Your holy name...

to show that You have played a role
in broken lives who've been made whole!

# FAITH LIKE DIAMONDS

I mourn in ashes and in dust.                    *Job 42:1-6
I pine for hope and grace,
when
I AM—                                            *Exodus 3:14
distant,
in my sin
between a Rock                                   *Matthew 7:24-27
and hard place.

So often
I don't want God's Word,
don't crave its sweeter truth.                   *John 17:17
I leave it abandoned
in my sin
as if Naomi had not Ruth.                        *Ruth 1:16-17

I pout
in darkening doubt,
and question God's commands.
I cry again from
in my sin
cause I don't like His plans.

Many times
I wonder
if there's Heaven,                               *Psalm 19:1-2
or even a Lake of Fire...                         *Revelation 20:10
thinking I know best
when more or less,
I'm calling God a liar.

Oh, Blasphemy!
That bitter pill,
I swallow in my haste.
In vanity of vanities,                           *Ecclesiastes 1:2
my soul's seems lain to waste.

But somehow...
in the dark of night
I call out in Christ's name,
longing for
His Open Door                                        *John 10:9-10
while the devil stakes a claim.                      *Job 1:9-10; 2:4

It is a brutal tug of war,
and I – the pawn like Job;
still my soul sings                                  *Psalm 96:1-3
as I will cling
to the hem of Jesus' robe.                           *Mark 5:25-34

This is just the desert sojourn,           *Numbers 32:10-13
that I must traverse now.
But though my soul's ship-wrecked,        *2 Corinthians 11:25
and my will's stiff-necked,                   *Exodus 32:7-10
let God burn my sacred cow!

Yes, grind it into powder, LORD!
Yes, scatter its remains!
Force me to drink the embers
of all my sin and shame!                             *Exodus 32:9-10

While pressed in this affliction, LORD,    *2nd Corinthians 4:8-10
do call the devil's bluff...                        *Job 1:12; 2:6
til faith, I find,                               *Matthew 7:7-8
and my soul shines                              *Matthew 5:14-16
like diamonds in the rough!

# FAMILY BUSINESS

We all know the rules
of supply and demand.
Our economy is based
on such golden plans.

What's wanted most
will sell off the shelf.
It's just a matter
of catering to wealth.

Something so beautiful,
trendy and new,
will catch the attention
of mankind, that's true.

But I have a grand Father
Who deals in junk,
and He has
moved mountains                                    *Mark 11:23
of scrap metal gunk.

His business is an eye sore
to some who come near,
for their eyes cannot see
and their ears cannot hear...          *Matthew 13:14-15

...oh the sound
of my Father's
raging fierce flame!          *Exodus 3:2, Hebrews 12:29
White hot,
but contained,
like a paintbrush so tame.

He takes those old metals,
so twisted and warped,

and molds them as finely
as David played his harp.

Until they become
some new--
in His Own image.
Works of fine art,
with no wrinkle, spot, or blemish.

And so,
me and Brother,
we go out to find...
more pieces
for Father
to mold in His time.

And I don't really know
much about what to do,
because I am too little--
see, it's Big Brother Who...

...can spot the right pieces
on His judgment, I rely...
because it's well known
that He has Father's eye.

So He can tell
the good junk from bad,
what can be recycled
from what
WILL NOT
be had.

And so Brother guides me
through mounds of trash--
keeping me safe from
the rats, snakes, and ash...

*Malachi 3:1-3
*1 Samuel 16:23

*2 Corinthians 5:17
*Genesis 1:27

*Ephesians 5:27

*Hebrews 2:11-12

...all for Our Father                                  *Matthew 6:9
-Who carries a torch-
for these pitiful pieces
in need of His scorch.

As He picks them up,
and blows the dust off--
matter will scatter,                                   *Ezekiel 22:15
while He wipes the must off.

He pulls down His mask
so we can't see His face,                              *Exodus 33:20
but we see all the sparks
from behind                                            *Exodus 33:23
as His grace...                                        *John 1:16-17

...is revealed in the most unlikeliest place,
when beauty emerges from ash and disgrace.             *Isaiah 61:3

It's not for the money,
Father's wealthy enough--
but He'll make His prophets
call the enemy's bluff...

...as if he has a right
to take Father's place...                              *Isaiah 14:12-14
steal, kill, and destroy                               *John 10:10
in a futile mad race.

Even still, we'll watch Father
weld more pieces together,
like a strong iron-cast quilt
to withstand the weather...

...some one hundred,
forty-four thousand
old odds and ends
will from an iron structure                            *Revelation 14:1

soon just within…
…a matter of time
and through reasonable measures,
as mankind's old trash
turns to                              *Ezekiel 18:30, Matthew 4:17
the Son of Man's treasures.

Author's Note:
As a child in the 1970's, my paternal grandfather owned a scrape yard known as "Whistler's Machinery & Supply" in Corsicana, TX. It was an EYE SORE. Nothing but mountains of old metal and junk. But my father, a man named, Alvie Lee Whistler, would find old pieces of metal to weld into elaborate and beautiful sculptures. When our father suffered a terrible stroke, and I moved home from Maryland to be with him for as long as I possibly could…there were mounds of rusty scrape metal all over our father's property. One day I asked my older brother why our father had moved all this junk metal into his yard. He told me, "See…some of this can be recycled, and Daddy knew which pieces to use for that." Granted, we are told in Scripture that there is nothing innately "good" about humanity. So there is is no "good junk" inside of us that can be found, apart from Christ. For example, we are told that our best works are like filthy rags before God. However, because it gave Him great pleasure to redeem us…to salvage us…from the mess we created in Adam's fall, we "turn to," meaning – we repent, to Christ. And God takes an old lump of junk through the refining, baptismal fire of His Holy Spirit's conviction and makes something *new*. Like the prophet Isaiah described, "…beauty for ashes."

# FATHER KNOWS BEST

some say God's not jealous,                          *Exodus 20:5
but I assure you

**GOD IS**

some say God's not zealous,              *Joel 2:18, Zechariah 8:2
but for His children

**GOD IS**

you say that you're bored
and tired of His Way,                                *John 14:6
that you want to go
to a friend's house and play

and so,
        He won't force you
His child,
        won't divorce you

He gives you
        *some free will*
            to decide

with whom you will go
but He wants you to know

He'll be waiting
        til you're back
            by His side

and don't be surprised
at the tears in His eyes
when some new
        *father figure*
            comes along

and him, you adore—
for his rules aren't a chore
but what
*he feeds you*
won't make you grow strong

that one lets you play
however you may...

out in the streets,
no buckles for seats

no homework, bedtime
no reasons, no rhyme
      and your wish will be his command
and whatever you say
is his rule for the day
      but for you, he won't take a stand

he's there to be "fun"
and your heart, he's won
      by telling you what you want to hear
but he does not care
about your welfare
      and has made that abundantly clear

then you come
      back as you please,
with broken bones
bloody knees
from a weekend of having
      *your own way*
without His Truth
for His Life to give proof
      that you would have been wiser to stay

some say God's not jealous,                *Exodus 20:5
but I assure you

**GOD IS**

some say He's not zealous                          *Joel 2:18, Zechariah 8:2
but for His children

**GOD IS**

and for this there are many good reasons
though times will change
and customs rearrange
He remains as a constant in all seasons          *Hebrews 13:8

so whether you love Him
or curse His name
this simple truth
is always the same

**GOD IS**

the beginning,
and

**GOD IS**

the end—                                    *Revelation 22:13
and He loves you so much
that His Son He did send...                        *John 3:16

to make it apparent

**GOD IS**

a faithful, *firm* parent

whose cross and its nails,                         *Galatians 3:13
proves His love never fails.              *1 Corinthians 13:4-8

# FIVE SMOOTH STONES

A giant looms over my head,
so what am I to do?
Shrink in fear
as he nears
and scatter like the Jews?

For they trembled at Goliath
with his javelin, spear, and sword;
how can I be
like David
and find faith in the LORD?

This ruddy, bright-eyed boy,
a youth so
meek and lowly...                                    *Matthew 11:29
this child of honest origin
whose stance was strong and holy—

he did not choose the armor,
or bronze helmet of a king;
just five smooth stones
and humble shepherd's bag and sling.

And so he slung a simple stone
and laid the giant down
with the name of the LORD
that did afford
him victory renowned.                                *1st Samuel 17

So who is my giant looming,
coming at me
in fierce gait?
Is he such a contender
that I scramble and I wait?

Is he a fear or circumstance?
Is he a burden, debt?
Is he a question
in my heart
or vainglorious need, unmet?

Is he a painful memory
or loathsome divination?                              *Leviticus 19:26
Is he a consequence of sin
from the enemy's machination?

Where are my stones
to sling at him?
In what brook do they lay?
And will I have
the strength to seek
God's name with which to slay...

this freakish creature
taunting me
this mammoth, goading hulk...
this, my cruel leviathan,                              *Isaiah 27:1
from which I cower, sulk.

For I am broken
as Israel,
I'm torn in two and spent.
I shutter at the sight of him
in shock that won't relent.

Take my eyes
and give them sight!                                   *John 9:1-25
Your glory, let them see!                             *Matthew 13:16
Fix them on
the CHRIST who saves,                                    *Acts 4:12
who calms the raging sea!                          *Matthew 8:23-27

And though
I am a gentile,
with no throne from which I came...
raise up this stone
though faith alone
as child of Abraham in Your name!                    *Matthew 3:9

Send me, LORD!                                       *Isaiah 6:8
And sink my aim
into forehead of my game.
Let giants fall
at this, Your call,
of which I am not ashamed.                           *Romans 1:16

For is there no balm in Gilead?                      *Jeremiah 8:22
Is there no prince of peace?                         *Isaiah 9:6
Is there still hope
for me, a sinner...?
Yes, there's a KING                                  *John 18:37
who *lives* in me!

# GOD, DIVINE

A stick, I take, and whittle fine,
just like my Grandpa told me
with his own knife,
and embittered wife,
another lesson that they showed me.

I'd sit with Grandpa
in the dark
of his kingdom spent, alone—
full of sawdust-schemes
and wasted dreams
lying
on his
humble blanket-throne...

where he was was cast
out of the house
for fear she'd smell his beer
and waken such a rage in her
of that
he truly feared...

"Don't tell Mama,"
when I, a child,
had seen forbidden fruit—
clad in his hand
inside the can
of aluminum ill-repute.

"It is a *sin!*"
This alcohol,
the beverage and it's scent...
that made him stumble
now and then,
...but giggle...
as he went

about his way
this day and that
bemoaning some great loss
like Ahab's illusive whale,
or some mariner's albatross

that hung about him
in a glare
of her nasty, vicious hate
as Grandpa put his fork
in meat right on top of my plate

being silly as a child
I tossed it on the table
with sole desire
to see him laugh
...as he was able.

That's when I heard
the spiteful words
she'd put into my mouth
~in chess, a pawn...
a hunter's fawn~
and conversation headed south,

"That fork has been inside *your* mouth!"
To imply I wanted no part...
of his stale breath,
*I died a death,*
cowering with him in my heart.

That anger there,
it was a snare,
like the sticks I'd learned to whittle
into serpents
of wood and stone                    *Deuteronomy 4:28
and gods that were so little.

But gods of mine
what are they now
that I am grown and gone...?
from all that fell
right into hell
of lives lost 'fore the dawn...?

of the Bright Morning Star                          *Revelation 22:16
that shown,
from a city on a hill...                               *Matthew 5:14
to beckon me
from a dark tree                                      *Galatians 3:13
and tell me to be still                                 *Psalm 46:10

and know the God
I cannot carve
from graven
sticks and stones,
from philosophic minions,
points of knowledge,
pompous clones
for nothing
short of His sound Word                               *Hebrews 4:12
can rise these old dry bones                    *Ezekiel, Chapter 37

from muddied waters' memories,
from a silent, screaming past
of broken words
and little ears that heard
the broken spirits' wrath

so breathe Your Word
into my soul
that I might be born again                               *John 3:1-8
and break this curse                            *Deuteronomy 5:7-10
for what it's worth
of ancestral, callous sins

that nag inside
the core of me
at times I can't transcend
the brutal aftermath
of tragic heroes lost and then

I look into a cloudy, vacant mirror          *1 Corinthians 13:12
...a void...
a wanting,
stirs in me
that cannot be quite clearer

than my desperate cry
as a young mother
with mounting bills,
and questions why

my family lived just as they had
and killed themselves too young...
so from the window of a van
one night
I cried, as all my hopes were hung

on this Jesus of Whom I read—
Light of the World                           *John 8:12
that shone,
and sheltered me
from wayward seas
calling to me that I'm known...              *John 10:14

And that to those who love Him,
and who keep His commands...
He will bless a thousand fold...
the generations from their hands.            *Deuteronomy 5:7-10

So gods of mine
they come and go
but not quite like this Wind                                        *John 3:8
that breaks into my conscious mind,
tearing down
what lies
within...

this Wind it rips through
a wood-filled forest
that I cannot see                                          *Matthew 13:13-15
          for trees—
which it uproots,
having no fruits,                                               *John 15:6
and brings me
          to my knees

on quaking ground                                      *Revelation 16:18
a waking sound                                          *Revelation 3:2
will shake me to my core...
as a trumpet's blast,                               *1 Corinthians 15:50-54
final cares I cast,                                            *1 Peter 5:7
passing through an open Door                                   *John 10:9

and fire consumes                                        *Hebrews 12:29
as pleasing fumes                                        *Ephesians 5:2
rise up to meet my LORD
from my sacrifice
of giving thanks                                            *Psalm 100:4
for sweet *grace* that He affords...                           *John 1:16

for all that comes to us
as a whisper, still and small,                             *1 Kings 19:12
for all He's done and doing still
despite the bitter fall                               *Genesis, Chapter 3

of man and wife
who toil in strife
      from lost love they forsake
from sin and death                                           *Romans 6:23
Sweet Baby's breath                                          *John 3:3
      resounds with calls to wake.     *Romans 13:11, Ephesians 5:14

And this I trust
so that I must
rise to walk in newness, sublime...                 *Romans 6:4
and let Him render
a heart so tender                                    *Ezekiel 36:26
formed by this God, divine.

# GOOD WORD OF GOD

What good are words we whimper,
that no one really hears?
What good are words we write,
if through them justice disappears?

What good are words we long be said
but are not, to conflict – stave?
What good are words we stifle
down and carry to the grave?

What good are words we 'oft repress
like "I love you" or "I was wrong?"
What good is pride                                           *James 4:6
if it should hide
our kinder side, lifelong?

What good are words that only
incite, but do not resolve?
What good are words we banter
'bout as relationships dissolve?

What good are words that whisper
just to fade like vapor off the tide?
What good are words held on
our tongue, hesitating to confide?

Good words are ones that will
age well in time like finer wines.
Good words are ones robust enough
to fill our hungering minds.

Good words are ones that spark
like fire, that penetrate in their role.
Good words are ones that leave us
breathless and can transform a soul.

Good words are ones that
take us back
and stop us in our tracks...
when toward the edge of mountaintops
we've wandered from our lack.

Good words are ones that grip us,
that do not let us go...
in an age of all politically correct
intentions, so wicked, we can't know.

Good words are ones that do convict
and haunt our conscious most,
reaping what we've sown                          *Galatians 6:7-8
through wordless groans                          *Romans 8:26
plead by the Holy Ghost.

Good words are ones that dawn on us
like some Bright Morning Star.                   *Revelation 22:16
And we can't evade
the cavalcade,
marching in
to kill our sin,
as He makes war.                                 *Revelation 19:11

So take those words and drink them
in their scarlet, scandalous red...
and brand your chest
with their stark letter
to tell the world you're His, instead.

And let them throw you hard
against the Rock of Ages,                        *Isaiah 26:4
but kiss their waves
as Spurgeon raved...
and die to sin and death's due wages.            *Romans 6:23

Then drink in these words and testify how
you've been healed by Christ's own scars,          *Isaiah 53:5, 1 Peter 2:24
that others might taste the fountain                              *Isaiah 55:1
of Living Water's rich reservoir!              *John 4:7-15, John 7:37-39

# GOODNESS

What is goodness?                                    *Isaiah 40:18
Or how can we define it?
Is it a smile
across the aisle
from casual friends
who shine it?

What is goodness
in this age
where all roads lead to home?
Is it some stone-wood statue, carved,
for bellies starved
of Bread                                             *John 6:35
and meat                              *1ˢᵗ Corinthians 3:2
who roam?

What is goodness?
Where's it found
when lost
inside our pain?
Is it in the eye
of storms we spy
from in the driving rain?

What IS goodness
after all, and how can it be measured...
'Gainst all the sorrow                          *Psalm 119:28
which we mourn                                  *Matthew 5:4
or joy                                             *John 15:11
that is our treasure?                           *Matthew 6:21

Goodness is in the earth                         *Genesis 1:31
and in the Light                                   *John 8:12
Who guides us.                                  *Psalm 119:105
Goodness is the fruit                        *Galatians 5:22-23

from mighty trees                                  *Isaiah 61:3
near still waters
right beside us...                                 *Psalm 23:2

But what is good
when all falls down
and crashes round our feet?
What is good when
we are pressed
beyond grand goals we cannot meet?

What is good
when deep inside
there seethes a deadly question,
"Does God exist
if I can't resist
vile sins that beg confession?"

I'll tell you where to find the good!
It is written
in a book,
one that mirrors us like the seas
and demands a closer look...

into our hearts                                    *Jeremiah 17:9
so sickened where
no goodness
ever blooms,
without He
Who parts the sea                                  *Exodus 14:21-22
sweetened                                          *Exodus 15:25
from the tree                                      *Galatians 3:31
He threw.

It's there where we
must till the ground
and ripen it for seed                              *Luke 8:11
that a Gardener                                    *John 15:1,
*John 20:15

hides,                                                      *Psalm 119:11
so the kernel dies;                                          *John 12:24
and sprouts the waving wheat.                          *Matthew 13:24-30

For goodness,
as defined by man,
is an answer to a prayer
only when we are granted every wish
our wicked hearts                                          *Jeremiah 17:9
can bear.

But goodness...
in the eyes of God,
is a fruit His Spirit brings                             *Galatians 5:22-23
to souls in trial
for a long while
through grief and suffering.                               *Romans 5:3

Deliverance is goodness,
but so is the journey spent—
as a bruised reed,                                         *Isaiah 42:3
with hungering need                                       *Matthew 5:6
that calls us to REPENT.                                   *Romans 2:4

And just has rain,                                        *Isaiah 55:10
falls not in vain,
but restores a dying earth...
and comes back not void                                   *Isaiah 55:11
or is destroyed—
nor will be the soul's rebirth!                            *John 3:3

Because we have a promise
bowed up in the sky, sublime!                          *Genesis 9:13-17
And for ears who've heard                               *Matthew 13:16
God's Holy Word
*is goodness...*
all the time.

# GRAIN OF SAND

this lowly speck,                              *Genesis 22:15-18
this grain of sand                             *Revelation 14:2
begs many waves                                *Hebrews 4:15
will understand…

a tiny pebble
loose in one's sock,
how do I
*dare*
confront the Rock…?                            *Psalm 95:1

the precious Stone
that lays in Zion –              *Isaiah 28:16, Romans 9:33
I am
a whimper
neath roars of Lion                            *Revelation 5:5

and yet I'm told
to boldly go                                   *Hebrews 4:16
before the throne
like wind that blows                           *John 3:8

cross wheat                                    *John 12:24
that's ripened in the field      *Matthew 9:37, Luke 10:2
like stars                                     *Genesis 22:15-18
that shine and don't conceal

the Light                        *John 8:12, Revelation 21:23
that breaks
from mourning's
glory
o'er sins
that tell our sorrow's           *2nd Corinthians 7:9-10
story

how can I share
for do I dare
approach this King, Most High                          *Esther 4:14-16
for I have sinned                                       *Romans 3:23
time and again
and deserve to die                                      *Romans 6:23

but instead of what
I'm due
He calms my savage seas              *Matthew 8:23-27, Mark 4:35-41
and gives me grace                                      *Romans 3:24
I cannot face                                          *Exodus 33:20
*rejoicing*                                            *John 16:20-22
on my knees

# GRAND PLANS

I come to You
with all my plans.
I claim to put them
in Your hands.

But do I ask                                    *Revelation 19:16
at all, my King,
what are *Your* plans
of which I sing…

from hymnals sweet
and newer songs—
does this heart,
to You, belong?

For if it doesn't                               *Jeremiah 18:1-12
then smash it, clean!
Like a clay pot,
this soul to wean…

from milk
to meat                                         *1 Corinthians 3:1-3
that I might feed
on what
this sickened heart                             *Jeremiah 17:9
might need.

Not for destruction,
wrath, or such…
but for Your divine
and gracious touch,

a vessel fit                                    *Jeremiah 18:4
to pour Your grace              *Ephesians 1:7, Colossians 1:6
in every land
for every race

and so my plans
what are they then...?
Best laid ones
of mice and men.

But You, oh GOD,                                              *Psalm 50:21
are far from me,                                             *Isaiah 55:8-9
higher in Your ways...                                      *Galatians 3:13
Your fruitful Tree

that raised up all my sin and shame      *Numbers 21:9, John 3:14-16
for me to see,                                             *Matthew 13:16
for fault to claim.

We go about our lives like this
in ignorance,
our state of bliss...

that we seem to truly cherish
for lack of knowledge,
and we perish                                                 *Hosea 4:6

seeking what cannot be found...
*peace*
in our own unsettled ground,

my lips have lied
when I say
I want Your Own
and not my way...

Gethsemane,
a cup not passed                                          *Matthew 26:36-39
and drops of blood                                         *Luke 22:39-46
a question asked...

Dare I look into His face?
To His wounds that give me grace?          *Isaiah 53:5, 1 Peter 2:24

And how can I presume that He
should offer more than this for me?

So all my schemes,
illusive dreams,
I place them on the cross...
let them die there,
like a serpent snared,
and see                                    *Matthew 13:16
I've nothing lost.

# GREATER HEALING

I'm crippled.
Can you see me?
Some say I haven't got a prayer,
and nor do I
for I oft' rely
on passers-by
if they're inclined to share.                                    *Acts 3:1-2

I often pine for a new life,
one in which I'm free to dance.
But no music sounds
where I lay bound
by bed sheets and circumstance.

These limbs have become heavy,
so much I feel I can't...
under their weight
and cumbersome gait,
I stumble,                                                       *James 2:10
thirst,                                                        *Matthew 5:6
and pant.                                                       *Psalm 42:1

It's true, this body's broken,
but more—
the soul within it, too,
for fears I can't shake;
dreams from I can't wake;
both overtake
no matter what I do.

And I have only weakened now,
contorted by grim fate;
as I surmise
the slow demise
of all for which I wait.

Where is my Bethesda?
No one has laid me near.
No angel stirs.                                             *John 5:2-8
Should I infer,
my faith - this God can't hear?

Is it just me
He does not see?
Am I left to be
laid out among the dogs?                                *Luke 16:19-31
What is the sin
I wallow in?
that I'm shunned from synagogues?

I'm crippled.
Can you see me?
Some say I haven't got a prayer.
Are they deceived?
Or should I believe
to what I cleave
and dare...

...not to bow
to sacred cows;                                   *Exodus, Chapter 32
to not curse God and die.                                  *Job 2:9
Yes, I'll hold fast
to Truth at last                                          *John 14:6
'til the Sweet By and By.

From my own eyes
I will take
the log that blurs my sight,                          *Matthew 7:5
and look toward
my GOD, My LORD,                                      *Isaiah 41:10
whose love is tough
-more than enough-                           *2 Corinthians 12:9-10
to humble me in plight.                  *James 4:6-7, 1 Peter 5:5-6

Though ailment torments me
so much I'd grown to fear it,
the God I love
lifts me above...                                      *1 Samuel 2:8
crushing sorrows of my spirit.                        *Psalm 34:18

For born of suffering and
things that cause us pain
is perseverance, character,
and hope that's not in vain.                        *Romans 5:3-5

There is a greater healing
than the sort we often covet...
but it starts
within hearts
where sickness breeds
so much we can't know of it.                        *Jeremiah 17:9

Christ is the Balm of Gilead;                        *Jeremiah 8:22
The Great Physician,                                  *Mark 2:15-17
of whom I boast.
And He has no ceilings                    *Mark 2:1-12, Luke 5:17-26
to limit healings
but cures eternally, foremost.

He who sits at God's right hand...                    *Hebrews 1:3
He who laid the streets of gold...              *Revelation 21:21
He's made a Way                                        *John 14:6
and place for me,                                      *John 14:1-4
tthrough His Own blood, Him told        *Eph 1:3-10, Col 1:19-20

Granted new life I've hoped for,
I'm called to take a stand...
at a Beautiful Gate                                  *John 10:9-10
whose Way, so straight,                              *Matthew 7:14
is the Son of God and Man.      *Philippians 2:6-8, Colossians 2:9

I was crippled.

Can you see me now?
Some said I had no prayer.
But I have seen                    *Matthew 13:16
my sins washed clean—                 *1 John 1:9
tasting                              *Psalm 34:8
true victory there!                 *1 John 5:3-4

# HEAR

tired of being tired
this soul the devil's priced...
and laid for me an offer
to see if I'll choose Christ

tired of suffering—
but of it, I will drink
tired of willful sinning
and the murk in which I sink

tired of everything
that used to sooth and ease us
tired of being more like me,
and less like God's Son, Jesus

tired and tired and tired again,
as one more time
I see                                             *Matthew 13:16
my sin...

that stares at me from a bloodied cross    *Num 21:4-9, Jn 3:14-16
and strikes my spirit cold,
from a grandma's lap
wake from the nap
and hear                                          *Matthew 13:16
her stories told

of a Sweet Savior
Who came for me,                                  *John 3:16
for you – lost world
hanging from that tree                           *Galatians 3:13

hear            *Matthew 13:16
The Revelation      *Revelation, Chapters 1-22
in her aged and straining voice
that spit hell in satan's face
should he dare to be my choice

hear            *Matthew 13:16
the subtle undertones
of a father's deep lament
for having chosen his own gods,
my damnation—him to prevent

hear            *Matthew 13:16
a sister's church invite
in a welcoming southern drawl
fear the demons it incites
but hear            *Matthew 13:16
the preacher's alter all

hear            *Matthew 13:16
the reason you did believe            *John 3:16
God's Word, opened your young hands,
recall the passion you received
with His Spirit and commands

someday hear            *Matthew 13:16
the worshiping cries of those
who wave palm branches in white robes      *Revelation 7:9

hear            *Matthew 13:16
the Master,            *Matthew 10:24-28
you tired slave            *1 Corinthians 7:21-22
among ones that He calls friend,            *John 15:15
and rise now from your dismal grave
and turn            *Psalm 34:14, Acts 3:19
from sin again

# HEART OF STONE

There was a stone
I'd left alone,
after casting                                          *John 8:7
as hard as I wanted.
But now it lay
like Potter's clay,              *Jeremiah 18:4, 2 Corinthians 4:7
no longer as a threat so undaunted.

It's fragile now, easy to break;
and as well it should have by now.
For I have carried it, stumbling…              *Proverbs 16:18
it was my sacred cow.                        *Exodus, Chapter 32

I'd put it on a pedestal
for all the world to see,
while I was being blinded
by its hate and tragedy.

Vengeance was not mine,
only God's divine.                              *Romans 12:19
And in sin
it had been
like a thorn stuck in my side.

But born of unmerited favor
I've been shown from holy places,
now I pray my bitterness
be turned to His sweet graces.

Like living water,                              *John 4:1-26
let them flow into a fount sublime!
And no longer numb,
let this stone
become alive
again this time.

So speaking of time,
I'm done wasting mine
knowing what I must impart...
with words, better said,
for my victim's not dead;
and no longer is my heart.                    *Ezekiel 36:26

# HOLY LABOR

God's bride                                    *Ephesians 5:22-33
has slept,                                     *1 Corinthians 15:51
while He's waited and wept—                         *Luke 19:41
    but death, now it has no sing...   *1 Corinthians 15:55
And I do strive
knowing she will survive
and will waken                                    *Revelation 3:2
    when called by her King.           *1 Timothy 6:15

For God is
    *JUST*                                    *John 5:30
    ...as a Servant—                   *Mark 10:44-45
    in all this time gone by.
And though the house
is unclean
that doesn't mean
    He's quit or hasn't tried.

He wore no fancy robes                    *Mark 12:38, Luke 20:46
from distant parts of the globe;
    He donned a servant's towel
and His hands did get dirty
washing feet                                      *John 13:5-15
cracked and hurting
    all with a smile, not a scowl.

And there is only one dress                    *Revelation 19:8
once perfect and pressed
    fit for a great wedding, that's true.   *Revelation 19:7-9
But now it's a mess
and no one will confess
    as to how
        it's been *stained* and *misused*.

Dirty laundry
piles high,
and He fields heavy sighs...
        one complaint after another.
He still comes to rescue
but pauses just to rue
        why we can't be more like our Brother?!     *Hebrews 2:11-12

But God is
        here to sweep away
        the ash
        from trays
        and to *scatter*
        the dust
        and matter
from tables---*turned*,           *Matthew 21:12, John 2:15
no lessons learned...

...and God is
by some ignored,
considered a bore

left stuffed in a shelf
*-beside Himself-*
while some family members
can't even remember
His heartfelt convictions
and painful afflictions
they disregard His opinions
and enjoy their dominion
over the earth
to whom He gave birth
and what was it worth
if not for His mirth...?

Since rain must fall          *Matthew 5:45
upon us all
from time to time
in His reason and rhyme...

if God is
in all His wealth                                          *Isaiah 33:6
still stuck in our shelves,
then we'll have to
pick up after ourselves.

For dirt will pile up—
passing plates,
      filthy cups                          *Matthew 23:25; Luke 11:39
          that cannot be filled,
by our own works                                    *Galatians 5:19-21
and anxious quirks
         until we can learn to be still...          *Psalm 46:10

and know
     what *Way*
        the *Truth* will stay
           with the *Life*                         *John 14:6
we are living:
for we must keep forgiving                      *Matthew 18:21-22
and stop reliving

all our past pain
that drives us insane,

but let it die on that tree                           *Galatians 3:13
so that we will see                                     *Matthew 13:16

that the force of His Living Water,                    *John 4:7-13
hot as iron being soldered                           *Malachi 3:2-3

will wash pain
down the drain
with no worry                               *Matthew 6:27; Luke 12:25
      to remain...

then keep on going
strong and growing
     like orchard trees
neat in a row
with fruit to show                     *Revelation 22:2
     that's grown ripe
          to disperse the seeds...      *Matthew 13:3-8

-so that the world-

...with hope diminished
can be replenished
from work that's been *finished,*          *John 19:30
complete—and as pure as Lamb's fleece.
Though consequences, infernal;
and housework, eternal;
strength comes from an internal peace...

...to surpass understanding        *Philippians 4:7
through troubles demanding
attention, time-spent, and tolls taken—

we'll have great delight           *Psalm 37:4
to fight the good fight         *1 Timothy 6:12
for the pride of God's joy
     when she wakens!         *Ephesians 5:14

# HOPE

Hope is a tiny budding thing
that breaks the ground in spring.
Hope is the wistful music notes
from cheerful birds who sing.

Hope quickens in the wombs
of those who nurture its frail life.
Hope stirs in them the strength
to carry its muster and its might.

Hope promises a future                                        *Jeremiah 29:11
when our dreams seem slow to wake.
Hope mounts on wings of eagles,                          *Isaiah 40:31
renewing strength should our souls ache.

Hope whispers in the soul
through wind and quake and fire;                     *1 Kings 19:11-13
though still and small,
Hope conquers all
of satan's guns for hire.

Hope defies the darkened shadows                       *Psalm 23:4
where demons sneer and bring
destruction to our spirits,
until death's told it has no sting.            *1 Corinthians 15:55-57

Hope stems from drops of mourning due,
when grief has learned its place.
Hope breathes the soul anew                          *Revelation 21:5
when God calls us into His rich grace.               *Ephesians 2:4-5

Hope lives inside a circle
when we feel broken and alone...
knowing angels praise
the God who'll raise
saints up before His throne.                        *Revelation 7:9-17

# HOUSE CALL

A little mess,
some here and there,
a pile of junk—debris;
At first
we do not notice it
'til we are
on our knees.

We ignore
the sight of it,
distractions
come and go
and we walk right through the filth
and it piles up and grows.

But soon before we know it,
disease has taken hold.
And we are ill,
for our own will,
has left us with a cold.

The virus hangs and feeds on us…
as it must run its course.
Make us shake and feverish
until the day we're forced…

to make a choice for life or death,
to rise or to succumb.
To face our fears
despite the tears,
knowing what we have become.

Accepting that in our own strength
there's never been a means,
to rid the grime
at any time
or hope to make us clean.

'Cept when we surrender
-let tumble down our walls-
for the Great Physician            *Matthew 9:12, Mark 2:17, Luke 5:31
Who has come
to make a *call*.                                        *Romans 11:29

# HOW HAVE WE PRAYED TODAY?

How have we prayed today...?
For all our wanton dreams...?
How have we prayed today...?
For all our desperate schemes...?

How have we prayed today...?
For happiness and wealth...?
How have we prayed today...?
For all success and health...?

How have we prayed today...?
Over statues that we've kissed...?
Knelt though doubt
with solemn pout,
giving God our laundry list...?

of things that He can do for us
to make our time here swell,
with milk and honey                          *Exodus 3:8
lots of money
oh,
and keep us out of hell.

We want so much.
We pine for it
until our bellies rumble,
but curse the bread                          *Numbers 11:4-6
on which we're fed
like Israelites who stumbled...              *Proverbs 16:18

in a desert wasteland
from which there seemed no relief.
How so, like we,
on bended knee
now question our belief...

in the God of Moses  
Who lays commandments down,                      *Exodus 20:1-21  
from Whom we turn  
and never learn—  
in fear that we will drown...  

much like all of Pharoah's armies  
in a sea of waves so red;                        *Exodus 14:26-31  
dreading that Christ can't  
calm storms,                                     *Luke 8:22–25  
feed masses,                          *Matthew 14:13-21; John 6:1-14  
raise the dead.                     *Matthew 27:50-54, John 11:38-44  

How have we prayed today...?  
To gods of little hope,  
to gods of comfort, ease, and things  
that simply help us cope?  

How have we prayed today...?  
To images so graven?                             *Exodus 20:4  
How have we prayed today...?  
As we're too good for food of ravens?            *1$^{st}$ Kings 17:6  

Yet Solomon prayed for wisdom...                 *1 Kings 3:7-14  
And Joshua, the sun, in battle...                *Joshua 10:12-13  
Paul for peace                         *2$^{nd}$ Thessalonians 3:16  
and Gideon, fleece,                              *Judges 6:36-40  
from the God who owns all cattle  

up on a thousand hills;                          *Psalm 50:7-15  
the sparrows as they fall,                       *Matthew 10:29  
the creeping things,                             *Psalm 104:20-25  
and brooks that spring...                        *Proverbs 18:4  
as wisdom brings  
righteous fear to one and all.                   *Proverbs 9:10

Have we now prayed today
with petitions such as these?
Or have we prayed today
for only what we please?

Have we prayed today
with requests, so cute and quaint?
Or have we prayed today
with the passion of a saint?

For what burdens me
is that this we see,                                    *Matthew 13:16
despite our joyful noise in chorus:                        *Psalm 98:4
God longs to do something *in us*…
before doing something *for us*.                          *Mark 2:1-12

# HUNGERING

Aggravation tears at me;
disgust has flood my soul.
No patient glee,
or hope to see,
a new day come unfold.

Failure looms at every turn;
I'm beaten in defeat—
mistakes, they mount,
such I can't count,
bitter blows from driving sleet.

I've made my bed, so lie in it.
I blame no one but self,
and while age weighs
depression stays,
as dreams wither on the shelf.

The sun is gone
and stars shine less.
Dusk steals another day.
I'm like a broken record
whining
that I've lost my Way.                    *John 14:6, Acts 9:2

*...what can I do?*
*...to whom to turn?*
When the weight of life
is falling
down on my weary shoulders
and I've lost sight of my calling?

Where are you, Hope?
Don't hide Your face                              *Psalm 27:9
with Faith and Love to follow...    *1st Corinthians 13:13

stranding me alone
with fate unknown,
in pity—left to wallow.

So many times
I have held on
against all of the odds.
I've smiled through pain,
and rage—restrained,
knowing that
there is a God.

But is He there
even now
when I am so broken, torn?
Has He forsaken me
and why...
as though I'm not reborn.                                   *John 3:1-21

There is a void,
a hollow shell,
I fear
where faith can scarcely reach.
What is this chasm?
This crippling spasm?
Can't I practice what I preach?

For I have thought myself
to have had
ears that heard,                                   *Matthew 13:16
so now it's time to hold again,
and wrestle God                          *Genesis 32:22-32
over His Word.

I am a tender reed,
so bruised and sliding back...
I am that smoldering wick
that threatens
fade to black.

Even so the prophet tells me,                           *Isaiah 42:3
this reed, He will not crush.
He says, no doubt,
Christ won't snuff out
this flame that wavers much.

Even so the prophet tells me,                          *Ezekiel 36:26
Israel was given a new heart!
Not one of stone
left all alone,
but of flesh—and set apart.

Even so the prophet tells me,                        *Jeremiah 10:1-16
not to live in a facade…
not to worship comfort,
my own works, and other little gods.

In there, the psalmist tells me,                         *Psalm 37:23
I will not be cast headlong
though I fall
if I do call
Christ will uphold me, strong.                        *Isaiah 41:10-13

In there, the psalmist tells me,                         *Psalm 37:40
to the LORD I must hold fast…
as my soul aches,
in refuge take
His promises fore-passed.

In there the psalmist tells me,                           *Psalm 37:4
in Him must I delight…
for saints aren't severed.
but preserved forever—            *Psalm 37:28, Philippians 1:6
like a city on a hill, shining bright!                   *Matthew 5:14

And now apostles tell me                             *Ephesians 6:10-17
to fix a breastplate o'er my core
'gainst fiery darts

aimed at the heart;
and be a slave to sin no more.                              *Galatians 5:1

And now apostles tell me,                              *Hebrews 12:11
that discipline will bring pain
but later yields
a harvest-field
of fruit                                              *Galatians 5:22-23
for those
who have been trained.

And now apostles tell me            *Romans 4:19, James 2:23
how much belief can count:
how Abraham
pleased the Great I AM;              *Exodus 3:14, Mark 14:62
like the sermon on the mount…                    *Matthew 5:1-12

assures me in Christ's Own Word
of just what God has willed:
that this vessel, void,                              *2 Timothy 2:20-21
won't be destroyed;
but with righteousness, so filled!                    *Matthew 5:6

# I AM A WRETCH

I am a wretch.
I know my sin.
Like cluttered filth,
I stumble in.                                        *Matthew 18:8-9

At times there seems
so little hope
of change in me
or ways to cope...

when in my spirit,
an anger burns;
a vengeance craves;
a lust that yearns.

These all divide
and conquer me
when I am tired
and cannot see.                                      *Matthew 13:14-15

They sift my soul
like so much wheat                                   *Luke 22:31
they leave me
barren
in defeat.

So take this clay
and pick it up,
then smash it fiercely down—
its vessel shatter                                   *Jeremiah 18:4
and pieces scatter
while crashing 'gainst the ground.

Yes, break this heart;
tear it apart
til
You are
satisfied…
break in me the spirit, wicked,
until
I am
truly tried.

Set me in the fire;
hold me Your vice…
melt, in me, impurities                                    *Malachi 2-3
and cut me with Your knife

Your blade as sharp as iron,                        *Hebrews 4:12
Your Word as hard as Truth—                          *John 14:6
and send me 'fore the lions;                  *Daniel, Chapter 6
let me seem to some, uncouth…

lacking in sophistication,
social norms,
and all that's polished:
let me reside
in You, abide,                                            *John 15:4
till lies are all demolished!

Break in me the ego,
the vanity of pride…                *Ecclesiastes 1:1, Proverbs 16:18
strip me of many vices
for from You, sin cannot hide.

You know this wicked heart of mine,
You see it's sickened state…                          *Jeremiah 17:9
so let Truth be heard
from in Your Word;
let me contemplate its fate.

I am a wretch.
I know my sin.
I see                                          *Matthew 13:16
death in its face...                           *Romans 6:23
but dry bones can live
with breath, God gives,                        *Ezekiel 37:1-14
and raise an army by His grace!                *1 Peter 5:10

# I SELDOM PRAY FOR MIRACLES

I seldom pray for miracles,
not because I don't believe.

I seldom pray for miracles,
for I hope not to receive...

blessings that I don't deserve
for I, have nothing done...

for that so precious of a grace
my human heart has won.

In me - there is nothing;
I am apart...undone,

save for my Master and His face
that's shone in Christ, the Son.

I seldom pray for miracles,
because, you see, I feel...

that if I pine for health and wealth
the enemy might steal...                                    *John 10:10

all the love I have for Christ,
without Whom – I'd be lost.

I seldom pray for miracles...
I have one...on the *cross*.                        *Colossians 2:13-15

# IN CHRIST

I am
in Christ,
all that I need…
He is
the bread
on which I feed.                                    *John 6:35

I am
in Christ,
a comfort – song…                              *Psalm 118:14
it is to Him
that I belong.

I am
in Christ,
all I can be;
because He bore
a shameful tree.                                  *Galatians 3:13

He took the sin
that separates
me from our God
and soothed His hate.                          *Isaiah 53:10

He came
as gentle Elder Brother,                    *Hebrews 2:11-12
though God in man—
He is none other.

So Him I hail
and Him
I love,
Sweet Son of man & God above.

# IN EVERY DARK PLACE

I'm having a mood,
trapped in a dark place.
I question the meaning
of life's chaotic race.

I continue on...
press into the day,
forging into submission
when night has its way.

I lean on dear friends.
I know that they care.
And I know that God hears
my fervent, dire prayers.

I am not alone
in these turbulent times.
Others suffer through losses
much harder than mine.

And I have learned,
time and again,
that we are blessed
most when heavy laden
for Christ gives our souls rest.

The LORD is our fortress                              *Psalm 18:2
in all wars ever started.
He is Gilead's balm,                          *Jeremiah 8:22
close to the broken-hearted.                    *Psalm 34:18

So I'll persevere
in spite of my pains,
and I will hold on
to the faith that sustains...

knowing for every rain drop
falling in this dark place,
that there is a sun ray                                    *Matthew 5:45
and the light of God's grace.                              *Acts 20:24
In Here, My Hiding Place

In here
this quiet place
door is shut
with windows, blinded...
...across the way
a mirror casts back                              *1 Corinthians 13:12
the dim-hued wall
and clothes are strewn
as a lamp's light fades
from near empty oil.                               *Matthew 25:1-13

Out here
this quiet place
I watch
the lemon-green April leaves
dawn on every branch
that sections up the sky
and yet...

-inside/out-

have all become so indiscernible
-interchangeable-
yet without change,
the monotony
of steel-gray, chain-link days
*twisted*
to form
yet another barrier
I cannot penetrate.

And in here,
this other
solumn assembly—
the seats are wide
with the Way
made more narrow                                    *Matthew, Chapter 23
than It is,
and *some*
of these windows—
blinded from being
*stained* so much,
that there is no
Son
in this dark place.

Yet I kneel,
with impending plea...for *what?*
"Just *something* somehow please
just *let me FEEL* again!"

Then alone
in prayer
through room after room
all vacant and hollow—
**it** does not leave…
**it** hisses…
**it** follows me…
with the pervading weight of nothing.
How can it weigh so much?

But in here
-this private torment-
a heart still beats
*as Life is breathed*
into my winter                                      *Song of Solomon 2:11
by lips unseen,
raised up                                                      *Psalm 145:14
by humble hands.

I cannot fathom
their strength
that lifts my
man-made cross
of nothingness
into oblivion.

And in here
my Hiding Place,                                        *Psalm 32:7, 91:1
I seek sweet refuge                                        *Psalm 18:2
that is found again
through such a
meek and lowly Spirit                                    *Matthew 11:29
Who lends a hand
to offer me
His
*blood-bought*
Rose
of Sharon.                                          *Song of Solomon 2:1

Author's Note:
This is a poem about the living with the struggle of clinical depression,
as I have experienced it. At times like these, the enemy colors our
whole perception of our surroundings – causing us to potentially
even loose hope in the church. But the all sufficient grace of Jesus
Christ that sustains us in the darkest of times...He comes to renew
our faith. He *becomes* our hope...when hope seems lost.

# IRON CAST HEART

A dust boy—clothes stained and ripped,
a wrought iron treasure in his grip...

just some rusty scrape he'd hoped to
mold to watch its inner beauty unfold.

So he hobbled in from the cold winter,
as crutches would creak and splinter...

Under the weight of this boisterous child,
whose bent frame from offset by his smile.

But before speaking to ask his dad
if this old junk metal could be had,

he heard words that would forever sting,
"Oh! He's *crippled*! That poor little *thing*!"

*"Crippled,"* he wondered, *"What does THAT mean?"*
Was it his legs? Was it the way that he leaned?

Despite good intentions that were had,
he just knew that it meant something BAD.

But he went about well on his way,
sorting through Dad's old scrapyard for play...

and taught himself how to do many things:
like welding bent nails into bowls for his King.     *Revelation 19:16

These bronze metal fruit bowls,
he would then turn
upside-down,
and weld on three crosses
for the One with the crown...                      *Mark 15:17, John 19:2

to honor the Lamb,                                        *1 Peter 1:19
more broken than he...
remembering him
on old Calvary.

A talent and patience this had required,
one that had been divinely acquired,

from his time spent bedridden in the past
and hours on end in full body casts.
But when the pain in his hip was too much
he'd pray for the LORD's invisible touch...

and it would come when the medicines had failed,
as strong and as sure as the bowls made of nails.

Then back good as new he would soon be,
up on his crutches and ready to flee...

and out to Dad's scrapyard fast like a fox,
this time to raid an old wrecker's glove box.

And a 1950's dictionary fell out on the seat,
so he blew off the dust to read in the heat.

*"Now what was that odd word
I was called on that day?"*
He wanted to see what
Mr. Webster would say...

"Crippled," he spotted on the
page with his finger,
and read it's meaning
as tears welled up to linger,

"A person or animal who is unworthy...unfit."
And he sobbed as this realization hit.

Despite all of his talents,
his mind, smile and cares—
all some people would see
were two crutches, wheelchairs.

An obedient child, no one
needed to scold him.
Never thought himself different...
until someone told him.

But that wasn't the only book he had read,
and defined himself by words written in red.

So the boy grew to be a man,
with grace and faith on which to stand...          *Ephesians 2:8-9

He learned to draw and lived to love,
to be my dad—now gone, above.

And on his stone is etched a creed,
a lesson that we all should heed:
The Word to Samuel
is what sets God apart...
though man sees only flesh,
the LORD looks at the *heart*.          *1 Samuel 16:7

# JESUS

We fell
and did you leave us there
beside a garden tree?                                    *Genesis 3:6-7
We died                                                          *Genesis 3:3
and did you ignore our fear—
choose not to hear or see?

Because our sins were heavy
up on that wooden cross,                           *Galatians 3:13
and yet You came and carried them
that we might not be lost.

You picked us up;
You heard our cries...
to You, they matter much!
Each falling tear,
each aging year,
Your joy expunging such!

This joy is strength,                                    *Nehemiah 8:10
our beckoning,
the rock on which we stand...                   *Matthew 7:24-27
to proclaim
the blessings
that have come forth from Your hand.

You take the weak
and make us strong.                                 *2 Corinthians 12:9-10
You guard against our shame.
You stand before the Magistrate,                    *1 John 2:1
invoke His holy name.

You say to Him,
"My brethren, I've absolved."
He counts us then as righteous
because YOU did *never* fall.

What is this grace?
What is this truth?
Pilate could not comprehend...                    *John 18:36-38
as You stood before his court
and would not flinch or bend,

to save Yourself
from agony,
from torment,
as a King...                                       *Revelation 19:16
telling Pilate
that he had no power,                              *John 19:9-11
telling death it has no sting.               *1 Corinthians 15:55-57

# JUST CAUSE

*Psalm 9:4

The Advocate
He pleads my case...
I cannot look upon
His face.

*1 John 2:1

*Exodus 32:20

For
I am
hidden
in the Rock
-set apart-
with all the flock.

*Exodus 33:21-22
*Matthew 7:24-27

And there I wait
and pine for Love
with grace sufficient
from above...

*2 Corinthians 12:9-10

this hellacious world
we know;
this pain we feel
this hurt in tow...

that snares and binds us
as we speak
from which there seems
no soon relief.

But in Him there is joy profound,
a truth so told, a strength renowned—

*John 15:11

that passes by...
while our heads bow,
through wind and quake and fire
their sound-

*1 Kings 19:11-12

God was not in them,
but we now see                                      *Matthew 13:16
a gentle Lamb...                                       *John 1:29
a hallowed Tree                                     *Galatians 3:13

A Shepard still,                                    *John 10:11-18
an open Gate                                          *John 10:9
Who stands before
the Magistrate                                  *Revelation 20:11-12

He speaks upon our own behalf;
He bids us bring the fattened calf,                 *Luke 15:22-24

and celebrate
a child's return...
a soul now saved,
a lesson learned.

And so to He Who
intercedes,                                         *Romans 8:26-27
I fall, I cry
from on my knees -

You saved me from immortal doom,
You came despite we had no room;                       *Luke 2:7

for You, forsaken, beaten – torn,
for sinner's sake, we wail and mourn!             *2 Corinthians 7:10

But *revel* in
Your risen state,
Right Hand of God,
this is Your fate:

Born as a man
from virgin womb,                                     *Luke 1:30-38
cast aside
within a tomb...                                      *Luke 23:50-54

to rise again,                                          *Romans 6:9
to raise the dead                                      *Revelation 20:3
to make us new,                                      *2 Corinthians 5:17
Your bride to wed...                                  *Revelation 19:6-9

on a white horse, Your eyes aflame
we all will see your written name...
as
"KING OF KINGS & LORD OF LORDS"
with rod of iron and a sharp sword...          *Revelation 19:11-16

And You'll rule not as a
Lamb Who beckons,
but as a JUDGE
          Who's come
                    to *reckon*.

# JUST WORDS

*1 Corinthians 4:20

Don't let them be
just words to me;
let them sink deep in,
that Christ did die,                                    *Revelation 1:18
and He, Most High,
has conquered death and sin.            *1st Corinthians 15:55-57

Don't let them be
just words to me,
an ancient tale of sorts.
Let them go out                                    *Isaiah 55:10-11
as rain gives sprout
to lend speech when called to courts.          *Matthew 10:19-20

Don't let them be
just words to me
to sooth the fear of death.
Let their seed                                    *Matthew 13:23
inside me breed
so I am quickened by God's breath.       *Psalm 119:25, Romans 8:11

Don't let them be
just words to me.
Let them baptize me with fire!             *Matthew 3:11
For I'm as lowly
as the earth,
but Your ways – like heavens
are higher.                                    *Isaiah 55:8-9

Don't let them be
just words to me.
Don't let me languish, rot.
For the lake of fire                             *Revelation 20:15
would soon acquire
my soul if they are not…

The Living Truth                                          *John 14:6
Who's come for me,                                        *John 12:46
the fount of life I drink.                                *Isaiah 55:1
The Bread from Heav'n                                      *John 6:51
sustaining me                                             *Psalm 54:4
in all I do and think.

Don't let them be
just words to me.
Let me run the race's full length.                   *Hebrews 12:1-2
Divided by the sword,                                 *Hebrews 4:12
loving the LORD
with all my heart, soul, mind, and strength.            *Luke 10:27

# KING HEROD'S LAST STRIKE  *Genesis 3:15

I watched a TV show last night
about abortion, our "*civil*" right.

      A sweet young girl lay
      on a table, chewing bubble gum,
      while a doctor—as requested
      used a machine that hummed.
      It ground and churned inside her,
      I bet it made her bleed.
      And she was shaken,
      crying endlessly.
      "It must have hurt," I cried
      *with her*
      while sitting home, unseen.

And I am
*angry* at King Herod               *Matthew, Chapter 2
who is now disguised
as the desperation
that's been
eating this girl alive.

You see, King Herod
drinks his wine, screams—
"All for me, me, me!"
He does not share with anyone,
it's good to be the 'king.'            *John 16:11, 2 Corinthians 4:4

And King Herod continues
to rear his ugly head
in third world famines,
plagues, and pestilence.

Then he visits every land
with needles and cocaine,

all targeted toward the children
just to see if they'll refrain.
Or maybe they'll fall
into his elusive trap...
overdose or HIV,
both prospects on his map.

I've learned King Herod                    *2 Corinthians 11:14
will change his form
from one century to another,
appearing out of nowhere
through some cause,
disease, or mother.

The children are God's favorite,          *Matthew 18:3-4
as we're told in His petition.
So every age this old King Herod
tries to squelch the competition.

You see, King Herod
is a *bastard*
of the lowest breed.                        *Genesis 3:14
He cons and wheels and deals...
and on our souls, he feeds.                 *1 Peter 5:8

You know,
I think he is *afraid*
that his reign
will soon be up.
I think he knows,

Someone is coming...                        *Revelation 22:12

with
Wine His Own                      *Matthew 26:28-29, Luke 22:20
to flow over
all our cups.                               *Psalm 23:5

# LAST CALL

greed is a thorn                                    *Luke 12:15
and pride is a thistle                              *Proverbs 16:18
but the trumpet's blast                             *Revelation 11:15
will blow the whistle

on grave mistakes
and past offense,
to reconcile
and recompense

the chosen few
from all the nations
with angels faithful
at their stations

and a call to alms
through glorious psalms
that have been written
by servants, smitten

with One so GREAT
     and yet so *meek*                *Matthew 11:29
Who will be found
     by those who seek             *Matthew 7:7-8

# LAST DAYS

Wolves come in packs,
thieves hide in dens—
quite in disguise
above all sin.

A multitude,
they do devour—
making a mockery
of Higher Power...                                        *Galatians 6:7

with crosses of wood & stone                    *Deut 4:28, Rev 9:20
-for looks alone-
they've crafted
into images so graven—
and truth lies
thrown
into the dirt,
coiled up and badly shaven.

Their nasty mess
has been confused
into our microphones,
as Judgment waits
at Heaven's gate
when wrath flies from the Throne.

But mighty oaks                                            *Isaiah 61:3
of easy yokes                                            *Matthew 11:30
stand firm against the quake—
no wind or hail
or tempest gale
can make their branches break.                            *John 15:5

Their stance is strong
with limbs grown long

and full of *fruit*,
      they render…
a wood grain
*new*
and fit for use
by quite a Great Carpenter.

Their roots runs deep
as Water seeps
up to outstretched ends—
to quench a thirst
for righteous works
and Truth,
they will defend…

…until the day
when the Son's Light may
outshine the dark campaigns,
      and renew
this world unglued
with His everlasting reign.

*Matthew 7:17; Luke 6:43-45

*2 Corinthians 5:17

*Mark 6:3

*Matthew 5:6
*James 2:14-26

*Revelation 22:23

# LESSOR LIGHT

*Genesis 1:16

In the mourning
of another day,
like any other
some would say...

as I revolve around my world
in the heavens, so free, unfurled

but hung within its gravity
its angst of total, grim depravity—

even still to me, this day is new;
as the Bright Morning Star                    *Revelation 22:16
does dawn right through...

the haze of pain that's hounding me;
the fog of lies surrounding me;

that says I'm gray and of no use;
that says my purpose hangs like a noose.

But this Star shows me how
to turn from all such sacred cows          *Exodus, Chapter 32

in clouded reflection—
divine perfection...

that only Christ can impute                    *2 Corinthians 5:21
to sinners like me, so ill-repute!

For when my God
does look at me
He will only choose to see
the Christ
Who outshines marks I've missed
and times I fell
while a serpent hissed.                          *Genesis 3:1

But now, so full, on harvest morn
my celestial body has been reborn!                 *John 3:3

And, therefore, all my work's now done,
knowing even moons reflect the Son.

# LET PURE SNOW FALL

as pure snow falls,
melts in the day;
as dark descends
with sinking rays
as petals wither
and dry with age;
as monies spent
to our last wage
as we fade
like photographs;
as kingdoms crumple
neath the wrath…

of God on high
who never lies;
who gives us life                                      *John 14:6
and testifies

that though we wrinkle,
pine, and pass;
seeing just a
clouded looking glass                          *1 Corinthians 13:12

for reflection
on our state;
to question
what's become our fate:

"A time to live…"
"A time to die…"                                   *Ecclesiastes 3:2
This time I'll call
on the Most High—                              *Psalm 91:1

asking to be a crystal of snow
that melts before His sight;
to be the dark relieved,
by now, His coming Light;                    *John 8:12

to be some dying petal
that dries into the earth;
to be the wealth—giv'n up
at my new birth;                             *John 3:3

to yellow into yesteryear
like a memory
caught off guard;
to fall like nations,
dashed to the ground so hard...             *Psalm 110:6

by a fierce, almighty Wind                   *John 3:8
that rages on—it's breath to send

an army from the old dry bones;              *Ezekiel 37:1-9
this spirit led and purged and honed...

to know this truth
from a serpent's pole:                       *Numbers 21:8-9
we loose our lives
to save our souls                 *Matthew 16:24-26, Luke 9:23-25

# LETTING GO

You were so small
when handed to me
-dark purple and still-
you barely breathed.

I hardly did, too...
while waiting to see
why you didn't cry
or move suddenly.

I held you tight,
I wouldn't let go
in that first moment
unable to know...

just what you needed
or how to find it—
that first of many moments,
if I could rewind it...

would I have you again?
Knowing how it's been...

so hard for you
in a world
you can't choose...

where crowds upset you
and people stare,
where words are like
a den of snares

that trap and snag you
in their maze,
while you wrestle
from a daze

they leave you hanging
on pieces gleaning,
as you struggle
with gestures for meaning...

something wanted
something found
something lost
or some strange sound

...has sent you wailing
high and low...
I hold you tight,
*I won't let go.*

How to ease your pain
I seldom know,
but I hold you tight
and won't let go.

I brace for impact,
weather the storm—
just to keep you
safe from harm.

But have you again?
Of course, I sure would!
For one of your smiles
shines like the sun *should*.

And for all of the blessings
that came by surprise,
as it was *through you* that
Christ opened my eyes...

and showed me the point
of life as we know it—
to lean on His grace,                    *2 Corinthians 12:9-10
letting His power show it...

to reach out to others
and to lift them up high,
not shrink from our problems
or shake fists at the sky.

And that's not to say
it's all been a breeze,
for I've spent many nights
bent down on my knees...

asking Him, "*WHY?!*
Was it something *I* did?
To deserve this lot,
what crime have I hid?

Have I passed down
my sin to *you?*"
I ask Him, "*Please!*"
That it's not true!

And in His Word,
I have found rest.                        *Matthew 11:28
It's so that He'll
be made manifest!                             *John 9:3

And that, He is
everyday—
when prayer and praise
chase fears away…

when JOY is found                              *Nehemiah 8:10, John 15:10-11
on cloudy days,
that is just when
I feel Him say:

"There's just one thing
that you should know—
I AM                                            *Exodus 3:14, Mark 14:62
holding tight,
I won't let go."                                *Psalm 145:14, Isaiah 41:10-13

Author's Note:
This is a poem about our daughter, her struggles with Autism, our
struggles, & the faith that has sustained us in the darkest of times.

# LORD OF ME

Be LORD of me,
oh God, my Christ.
Slay in me
all You despise.

For many will come
to You in that Day,                                    *Matthew 25:41
professing to have known
You and Your Way.

And they, You'll turn,
From Heaven's frame
'spite works in vain
done in Your name.                                     *Matthew 7:21-23

And like such I wonder
if I'm full or hollow...
if it is Christ, who I do follow.

But for righteousness,
I hunger, I crave.                                     *Matthew 5:6
So rejoice o'er me,
Mighty One who saves!                                  *Zephaniah 3:17

Soothe me with peace Your Spirit grants.      *Philippians 4:7
For You
is Who,
I pine and pant!                                            *Psalm 42:1

When satan lies,                                            *John 8:44
keep sin at bay...
crush his serpent head                              *Genesis 3:15
and have Your Way:                                         *John 14:6

when anger drives me
through and through...
speak, so waves of rage subdue;

when I am blind                              *Matthew 15:14
to my own sin—
touch my eyes,                                 *John 9:1-6
let see,                                      *Matthew 13:16
again;

when my faith dies
like old dry bones,                          *Ezekiel 37:1-9
breathe it to life
from God, Your throne;

when in affliction's furnace,          *Daniel, Chapter 3
almost faint...                 *2 Corinthians 4:1, Galatians 6:9
draw by me near,                                *James 4:8
so others hear                             *Matthew 13:16
perseverance of the saints.                *Romans 8:28-39

Be LORD of me—
heart, soul, and mind!                    *Matthew 22:37
Perform in me
a work divine!                            *Philippians 1:6

Wrestle me,
as You did Jacob,                        *Genesis 32:22-32
o'er his hip.
And be honored by my all...
not just my lips.                          *Matthew 15:8

# LOST AND FOUND

Have you ever tried
to cry
*but can't*
because
you're dead inside?

Have you ever wanted
and found
but can't receive…?
Have you ever felt a loss
that you cannot grieve?

Have you ever been made the fool,
been taunted, lost, alone?
Have you ever called for help
when no one gets the phone?

Have you ever felt
the need
to bleed…
but can't
because of scars
that all restrain
a flood of pain
brooding quietly in the dark?

Maybe it's the hurt
you've held on to for so long?
Maybe it's unforgiveness
'gainst one who did you wrong?

Maybe fate has come to your door
and placed a darkened wreath?
And maybe it has wielded
too much power
and broken all belief?

This death inside, this darkness where
no sign of life can grow...
so that it seems
no point to dream—
yet there's Someone you should know.

Some tell you He's
a lunatic,
or liar,
as they claim...
Some say it is a myth
He rose the dead                                        * John 11:40-44
and healed the lame.                                   *Matthew 9:1-8

But I have seen His power
in ways I can't describe
with just mere words
you've only heard
me struggle to provide.

He's calmed the tempest sea in me;                     *Matthew 8:23-27
He's quenched my longing thirst;                       *Matthew 5:6
He's driven out the demon's seed
tormenting my soul worse...

than a thousand nightmares
like the legion at Gerasenes;                          *Mark 5:1-20
He's given sight                                       *Matthew 13:16
to eyes that fight
back tears
as there's no means...

to aptly 'scribe His glory,
His Presence and His grace
that saves a sinning soul,
makes whole,
and lifts a tear-streaked face.

Yes, know He is the
The Holy One
who comes to captives, frees us.                    *Isaiah 61:1-3
Know that He reigns                              *Revelation 22:1-5
and souls, sustains,
and that His name is Jesus.                        *Matthew 1:21

# MAKE ME LITTLE

Make me little
that I may see.                                   *Matthew 13:16
Keep me humble,                      *Matthew 23:12, 1 Peter 5:6
hear my pleas.                                      *Psalm 17

Make me little
and still, to be                                   *Psalm 46:10
less apt to stumble                               *Jude 1:24-25
while on my knees.

Make me little,
clinging to
the Vine                                            *John 15:1
that bears in me much fruit.                         John 15:5

For weeds pop up                           *Matthew 13: 24-43
and strangle those
who don't abide
in Sharon's Rose.                          *Song of Solomon 2:1

Make me little
as a child—                                        *Mark 10:15
and tame in me
this spirit, wild.

Make me suffer                        *1 Peter 5:9-10, Romans 5:3-5
to give You praise;
as blind men see,                                   *John 9:25
and dead are raised.               *Ezekiel 37:1-10, Romans 8:11

Lead me straight
in the narrow
Way                                          *Acts 9:2, 24:14
that few will ever find.                           *Matthew 7:14
And count me righteous

by the blood
of Christ,
Who is divine.

While in the valley
comfort me
within Your staff and rod.
But make me little
hungering aft'
and fearing God.

*Romans 5:9

*Psalm 23:4

*Matthew 5:6
*Psalm 111:10, Proverbs 9:10

# MAKE WAY FOR BABY! *Isaiah 40:3, John 1:23

He's been waiting patiently
for many months so long.
He's been nesting nice and cozy
in His womb and growing strong.

And now He has decided
to come tearing out--
through cramping muscles,
burning flesh,
and spines that splinter into!
He'll leave us shaking, trembling,          *Philippians 2:12-13
'fore His glorious task is through!

But I wonder if He'll be upset...
or angry at a few
of His well-intentioned relatives
for whom
He's overdue.

For some haven't been prepared
to make an offering,
to welcome Him into this world
for all His suffering.

Some haven't been excited
about His soon arrival...
instead we've wondered if
He'll inconvenience our survival.

"Will this Baby hurt us...?
Will He demand too much...?
Time and money spent
toward all His needs and such...?"

"Will Baby make us miserable
living on the
straight and narrow...?"                    *Matthew 7:14
Well, misery does love company
with every fallen sparrow--                  *Matthew 10:29

into crime and rape and vicious lies
that lead us to the hearse.
I think it's safe to say,
without Him,
we've done worse.

I bet we'll be relieved
to see what joy                              *John 15:11
Baby brings...
see Him forgive
our sins,
our stains,
and all our shortcomings.

We'll see Him comfort and love us
despite the way we are...                    *Romans 5:8
if we repent
He'll wipe our eyes                          *Revelation 21:4
from wrongs made near and far.

And now at last – He's coming!
I feel my sides seize up!
But for all my crippling pain
it can't compare to this, His cup.           *Matthew 26:39

Can't others feel this pressure
in all surrounding areas?
Surely, I'm not the only
sainted mother                               *Galatians 4:19
in hysteria.

So soon, sweet rapture,
we'll see His face--
all else will melt behind Him.
All fear and doubt and agonies,
His touch
will bless and bind them.

This Baby offers love,                                    *John 3:16
it's what He comes to share...
along with peace eternally--                            *John 14:27
if our own cross, we bear.                          *Matthew 16:24

Author's Note:
In writing this poem years ago, I was moved by two things: the
"rebirth" of the human soul; and the return of Christ to this world.
Right now, perhaps more than ever, this world seems to be in the
beginning of sorrows, birth pangs...something that I, as a mother,
am well familiar with. This world is gripped – torn between its
selfish wants and the "Child" that came so long ago and Who will
come again. The world labors...fearing the demands this Child will
bring, just as young first time parents always do a little, no matter
how much the child is wanted. The pastor who introduced me to
the Christ decades ago would always say that before salvation we all
have this sense of "LORD...not yet. Let me have my life for a little
while longer." But we all have to come to terms with His decree, that
he who keeps his life will loose it...eternally. And truly, the kind of
love we humans know is not all that will be expected of Christians in
any age. We can "love" our dog or that perfect cup of coffee. Human
love can be very self-serving and conditional, subject to change when
we have been wronged or when we are simply distracted. But when
Christ saves us, it is not our own love that we will be compelled to
share, but His. And His love is deep, vast, and wide: deep enough
to quench all thirsts, ease all pains, and lift all spirits; cast enough
to span the universe and wide enough to span the cross. As such,
His love will not allow us to ignore the lost and suffering. His love
will sustain us to carry a *cross*. He will ignite a holy, consuming fire
in us – and with it, we will light the nations.

# MANKIND IS JUST

Mankind is just a whimper,
a brooding whisper in a crowd,
through many screaming voices
of those so led astray and proud.                    *Proverbs 16:18

Mankind is just a vapor,                              *James 4:14
some distant scent within the winds,
who toils only to die
after all the time he spends...

reeking havoc with his neighbor
whom he's been called to love,                       *Matthew 22:39
finding fault in every blessing
that's been sent from God above.

Mankind is just a photograph
that's been aging for a time,
and fading into yesteryear
used up and past his prime.

Mankind is just a hollow noise,
a gong or clanging symbol,                            *1 Corinthians 13:1
that howls in protest
'gainst the night and
never stops to tremble.                               *Philippians 2:12-13

Mankind is brief
like mourning due
o'er sin and grief
that he should rue.

But in the ashes of his shame
through turning to holy trust;
we find he's given a new name                    *Revelation 2:17
and transformed from clay and dust...

into a brilliant specimen,
a beam of Heaven's grace!
So now our God in Heaven
doesn't have to turn His face...                 *Isaiah 59:2

from arrogance, pride, and envy
from murder, death, and lust
from all mankind seemed doomed to be...
for now, through Christ, we're JUST.             *Romans 5:1-2

# MOURNING SONG

I stare into a white abyss,
not knowing what to say,
as writer's block
defies the clock
and wastes my time today.

I want to share a message
of hope and truth and grace.
But what is left, or right,
to write
when God has turned His face?                    *Isaiah 59:2

Or so it seems
to me at times,
when I'm alone and tired…
when dreaded quiet
precipitates
shots of remorse, now fired.

How is it peace
can trigger me…?
Ignite all of my rages…?
Leaving me to stare,
can't cast my cares,                              *1 Peter 5:7
harboring sin and all its wages…?                *Romans 6:23

I am not Abel,                                    *Genesis 4:4
in a play – but cast,
in the world,                                     *1 John 2:15
on all its stages.
I'm just a starving artist
now begging water                                 *John 7:37-39
from the Rock of Ages.                     *1 Corinthians 10:4

And so without my inspiration,
without my rhyme and muse...
I curse the day
and cry the night,
feeling I've nothing left to loose.

But yet there are...
the gentle hymns,
that charm my weary soul;
their fragrance sweet
and beckoning
when life has taken toll.

I sing them now
their melody—
their still, small whispering coo;
quite like a Dove...
it leads me now to
pastures green                                                          *Psalm 23:2
and new.                                          *2 Corinthians 5:17, Revelation 21:5

I follow
aft' their lingering...
their firm and fervent psalms;
for even Judah made amends,                                *Genesis, Chapter 38
even Gilead has a balm!                                            *Jeremiah 8:22

I sing these praises to my God
though faith is weak is dismal;
I cry to Him
though obedience has been
so lacking and so bismal.

And taste bitter
salt of the earth
from tears that stream, so sour.

I stop
and turn,
confess my sins,
knowing now such tears have power.

For where repentance leads
is into Godly sorrow:                              *2 Corinthians 7:10-11
and from it blooms
life from the tombs
and mercy for tomorrow.                          *Lamentations 3:22-23

# MY PRECIOUS JESUS

There was a time
I thought I knew
what was right
and what was true.

There was a place,
I knew mine well…
where safety meant
don't ask, don't tell.

There was a mold,
a shape to be—
and I, cut out,
to nth degree.

There was a wind
through raging limbs,
dark as the dust below…
and gray-toned as ashes in lament,
such sorrows, I did know.

There were gusts
of lusts
in mad downpour…
that were never quenched
in their foul stench,
but left me wanting more.

Caged in—
surrounded,
by glass walls that
I had built up on my own…
dare I lashed
to crash
them on that heart of stone?

Where was my Way                                                 *John 14:6
that once was plain,
where life was good
and right as rain?

Where was deliverance
from death's grim valley,                                     *Psalm 23
where lurked a thief—                                  *John 10:9-10
my debts to tally?

Where was my beacon,
my ray of hope,
sent shining through profound night…
to keep me on
the narrow path                                      *Matthew 7:14
that I might fight the fight?                        *1 Timothy 6:12

It could not come
from within me,
for there no glories save.
But I knew to seek                              *Matthew 7:7-8
One great and meek                            *Matthew 11:29
who's crushed sin and the grave.          *2 Timothy 1:9-10

He broke the mold I once was in.
He dawns a Light we can't out run.                    *John 8:12
And in Him all of my worries flee.         *Matthew 6:25-34
The devil's plans are all undone.

He took these all upon Himself:
my sin, disgrace, and shame;
and died with them up on a cross,     *Galatians 3:13, 1 Peter 2:24
but rose that I might know God's name.

He is the Calmer of my storm.                 *Mark 4:35-41
He's the Great I AM               *Exodus 3:14, Mark 14:61-62
who frees us.                                      *John 8:31-32
He is the Savior of the world.                   *Acts 4:11-12
He is…my *precious* Jesus.

# MY SURRENDERING

Take all that's in me that You hate,
and crush it for You Kingdom's sake:
vanity                                    *Ecclesiastes 1:2
and selfish pride,                        *Proverbs 16:18
anger,                                    *Ephesians 4:26-27
lust—                                     *1 John 2:16
my soul divide,
split it clean
and make me whole,
that I may someday
play a role...

in Your grand and Great Commission       *Matthew 28:16-20
to call a world for sin's remission.     *Matthew 26:28

For all who knock, You open doors;       *Matthew 7:7-8
and all who ask, You've given more:      *Matthew 25:29

as Sarah laughed in her old age—
You gave a son, nations, to raise.       *Genesis, Chapter 21

as Moses begged to stay your wrath       *Exodus, Chapter 32
from Israelites who chose a calf...

as Joshua spoke, the sun stood still;
and moon did stop, all at Your will...   *Joshua, Chapter 10

as Gideon asked for dew-filled fleece,
You showered it and gave him peace...    *Judges, Chapter 6

as Ruth clung to Naomi—*spent*,          *Ruth 1:16-18
You gave her Boaz of royal descent...    *Ruth 4:13

as Samuel said, "...Your servant hears..."
You prophesied & drew him near...        *1 Samuel, Chapter 3

as Elijah fled and made his choice,
You came to him in a still, small voice!                    *1 Kings 19:11-12

So search my heart and soul and mind—                      *Psalm 139:23
and give me grace, oh God, divine.
Open my eyes                                               *Matthew 13:16
and these wounds, bind;                                     *Psalm 147:3
for
I AM
seeking, sure to find...

a *treasure* hidden in a field;                            *Matthew 13:44
a *pearl* of price no one can steal!                       *Matthew 13:45

For, as I delight myself in You,                            *Psalm 37:4
You will
*change my heart*
and make it true...

to Your Holy Word and Him, alone,                          *John 1:1-4
that I cast all crowns before His Throne!              *Revelation 4:10-11

# NIGHT

Night pours down
and cools the day.
The earth is calmed
with stars at play.

Night brings sleep
for many –
but few                                    *Matthew 7:14
will wake                                  *Ephesians 5:14
to catch the fresh, clean dew...

of morning in its
golden splendor
from the sun,
its distant sender.

But it is night
who brings a quiet,
unlike the day's
chaotic riot.

Day can be a glorious place
where we plan and scheme;
but night's the one
who falls on us,
and slows the soul to dream.

It's night who
stills us
in his hush;
his blanket calm,
his silent touch.

And in the day,
who pines

to see? *Matthew 13:16
Or who dares bow down on
bended knees?

With paths so lit
and journeys unfurled...
who craves the bright
Light of the World? *John 8:12

Though day is full
of purpose, awed...
it's night
who brings us
close to God.

# OH, TO WAIT IN FAITH

Like earth pines for a sunlight morn;
like a deer pants for the brook;                    *Psalm 42:1
like the soul craves to be reborn,                  *John 3:1-3
I wait for God to look...

at me, in this: my wretched state—
my wayward, brooding dreams.
I contemplate
what is their fate...?
through all my desperate schemes.

What are my motives, God of mine...?
Are my ambitions true...?
Search my heart—
*sick*,                                             *Jeremiah 17:9
set apart
its inward groaning rue.                            *Romans 8:26

What is my purpose in this world?
What do I want from You?
What more is there
than a cross to bear                                *Luke 9:23
since You have made me new?                  *2 Corinthians 5:17

But Solomon asked for wisdom,              *2 Chronicles 1:8-12
and this You chose to bless.
You removed all our transgressions
from the east and to the west.                      *Psalm 103:12

Joshua told the moon to stop;
he told the sun, "...stand still..."                *Joshua 10:12-14
and it was so
ages ago,
all at Your given will.

And what of all the patriarchs
who died in their belief,                          *Hebrews, Chapter 11
but held hope high
under the thigh                                    *Genesis 24:1-4
from a promise, sure to keep?

As Rahab begged for kindness
and as she hid the spies;                          *Joshua 2:8-14
by a scarlet cord,                                 *Joshua 2:15-24
fear of the LORD,                                  *Proverbs 9:10
like such—my hope defies...

all reason, pomp, and circumstance;
all odds it's stacked against...
all nay-sayer's valore;
and all fear that I have sensed.

Would You use me, God of mine,
in Your Kingdom's quest?
For Isaiah's plea,
"Here I am. Send me!"                              *Isaiah 6:8
Weighs heavy on my breast.

Like Rebekah's love for Jacob
played well into Your hands,                       *Genesis, Chapter 27
let my life shine                                  *Matthew 5:14-16
as gold refined                                    *Malachi 3:3
by following Your commands.                        *Matthew 22:37-39

For when Abraham pined just for a son,
You gave a kingdom of stars and sand!              *Genesis 22:15-18
So lend me Your grace                              *2 Corinthians 12:9-10
to run the race                                    *Hebrews 12:1-3
and faith that will withstand...

while I wait for you, oh God,                      *Isaiah 40:31
and while I pine and pray
let me mount up like an eagle
weary not
to serve Your Way.                                 *Acts 19:23

# OLIVE BRANCHES

*Romans 11:24

A burning bush,
handwritten wall,
a raving man
we once called Saul...

*Exodus, Chapter 3
*Daniel, Chapter 5

*Acts, Chapter 9; 13:9

his words to Rome,
Esphesians' note,
still Word of God
whispered
by rote.

And so - a question,
popped in time,
in answer to
that age old crime...

of Eve's for listening far too close
to voices other than the Most

*Genesis 3:1
*Psalm 91:1

great kniving sword
that cuts us clean...

*Hebrews 4:12

the pain, we feel,
but Truth is gleaned!

*John 14:6

It separates my mind and heart,
my world it rocks & tears apart...

...sweet cunning lies
down to my marrow,
as I,
the falling of all sparrows,
but saved by God
& ways made narrow!
Along this road,
I take a harrow...

*Matthew 10:29

*Matthew 7:14

and till the ground
to make it supple,
for seeds of faith                                    *Matthew 13:1-9
with which to couple...

the emptiness, we are, alone
-apart from God, so unatoned-

but haunted by a Holy Ghost,
Who begs us pause...
Whose grace we host...

entertaining angels, unaware -                        *Hebrews 13:2
that it is He,
from Whom they share

a gracious smile, a loving heart
that judges not, but sets apart

the purpose of a smooth white stone,                  *Revelation 2:17
that's offered - costly - from the Throne...

the Father's love,
the Son He sent...                                    *John 3:16
a daughter,                                           *Zechariah 9:9
lost, who won't repent
but wails and cries,
her virtue spent...

as evil rears it's ugly head -
forever asking,
*"Hath God said...?"*                                 *Genesis 3:1

But still He holds an outstretched hand
a question posed, an offer stands...

Come take His now, Sweet Child of Zion,
Come hear the roar of Judah's Lion...

and Him alone, a stranger not,                                    *John 10:5
for Who has died and risen – thought...

you were His bride and are yet still;              *Ephesians 5:22-33
for *you* His pilgrimage and will...

compels you, stinging night and day,
like a love lost, once gone astray...

but fated now, sweet destiny
to see and hear                                             *Matthew 13:16
Him, Groom to be.                                    *2 Corinthians 11:2

And not for Zion, all alone,
but for the gentiles' old dry bones...          *Ezekiel, Chapter 37

that rise to everlasting life,
comprising now His wakened wife...              *Revelation 19:7

who will in full, sweet virtue be...
and taste the fruit                                       *Revelation 22:2
of Calvary's Tree!                                           *1 Peter 2:24

# ONCE AND FOR ALL

Once and for all—
please God, do call.
Once and for all,
help me stand and not fall.                    *Proverbs 16:18

For time and again,
I stumble in sin...                             *Matthew 18:6-9

then claim I'll do better
right down to the letter.

But I drift even more,
like a ship tossed offshore.                    *Ephesians 4:14

Like this I've so wandered
from the Master I serve,
feeling it's all been squandered...
the grace I don't deserve.

He's raised the dead,          *Luke 7:11-17; 8:41-56, John 11:1-44
and made blind men see.                           *John 9:1-25
So why won't He fix
the mess that's me?

Once and for all,
let me answer His call.                          *Isaiah 6:8
Once and for all,
let me stand and not fall.

For my ears have heard                          *Matthew 18:12-14
of a sheep in His herd,

who would stray until lost
as He counted the cost.

"Of a hundred, what's one,
in case it should scatter?"                                    *John 10:12-14
Might say a hired hand,
but to Christ we all matter…

enough to leave the ninety-nine others,
and reunite us with sisters and brothers.

So once and for all,
I will stand and not fall.
Yes, once and for all,
I will come at His call.                                       *John 10:27

# ONE FLOWER FOR THE GRAVE

A poem my Late Father, Alvie Lee Whistler

I saw my father's grave today          *Ecclesiastes 12:7
no flower's
fragrant breath
could breathe new life          *Genesis 2:7
below the grass
and bring him
back from death.

I saw my father's grave today
no flowers
did I leave.
There are not enough fields of them
to match the loss I grieve.

I saw my father's grave today
no flowers
by my side,
and fake ones
cannot imitate
the love I feel inside.

I saw my father's grave today
before rushing out of town,
with the kniving agony
that I
*had left him*
in the ground.

What is it like beneath the earth
encased inside a box…
where back to ash and dust,          *Genesis 3:19
we fade into the rocks?

How can I leave him lying there
and simply
drive away—
as if he doesn't need my care
or someone just to stay...

and shelter him from all the cold,
the storms that winter sends?
And who'll be near
with hope to hear
his whispers in the wind?

What is my prayer
with him now gone?
What claim can my faith own?
I am not strong enough, myself,
to roll away the stone.                                    *John 11:39

But in the earth that covers him,
seeds feel on fertile ground—                       *Matthew 13:8
with sun and rain                                        *Matthew 5:45
to nurture them
until the spring abounds.

So I will watch his grave each year
with eager, steadfast urge...
to see what budding
*Vine*                                                        *John 15:1
will come forth                                            *John 11:43
and emerge!

Since I am known
by One Who says,
"...the dead will rise from tombs..."              *John 5:28-29
I only have to wait until
my sweet
Rose of Sharon                                            *Solomon 2:1
blooms.

# ONLY HOPE

What is left to hope for,
and what is there to say…?
When all my plans
have shattered
and I will not have my way…?

What happens when I pray to God
and it seems He never hears,
through all this faithful service
in all the trials and years…?

Where do I turn;
what's left to learn…?
when hands are tied
and dreams have lied…?

When
I am
broken, destitute;
when
will is gone,
no resolute…?

When all that falls is
mourning due
in a cold thin spray
of gray-dimmed hue…

where aspiration drowns in rain,
and loose their aim as a weather vane
that spins and creaks within the storm
from winds that rip and warp its form…

when I am lost
in this foggy haze,
I'll bow my head in prayer;
and know the
One Who
calms the sea
is quietly waiting where...

my dying will
and all I cherish
of this life
will finally perish;                                    *Ester 4:16

where I submit all visions, schemes,
up to this One Who saves;                          *Matthew 1:21
and let them die
like kernels lie                                        *John 12:24
'side a thousand wheat seed graves.

For in the clearing
when harvest comes—                                 *Luke 10:2
like a pup begging of its Master, crumbs;      *Matthew 15:27
and all my striving tallied, summed,
while I wait to hear the angel's hum...

oh, just let me *hear*                               *Matthew 13:16
"Well done, thou good and faithful servant,"    *Matthew 25:21
as Jesus draws me near.                                *James 4:8

# ORDINARY

Sometimes I feel so unequipped;
so helpless...
even broken, stripped.

I wonder what to do,
which path to take
or stay
I wonder if I'll ever crawl
out of trouble and dismay.

I read of all God's patriarchs,
their passion and their strife...
question my faith,
examine it,                                    *2 Corinthians 13:5
in this ordinary life.

I have to wonder
if I'm true
if what I want is real...
when so oft' I am a prisoner              *John 8:34
of what I think and feel.

Do I submit to You,
oh God...?
is it Your will and reason
that governs mine
for oft' I find
myself in boredom's season:

no winter wind to chill me cold,
no springtime breeze abounding...
no summer's heat to set aflame,
no autumn tones resounding...

with almighty emphasis;
just one day then the next
of ordinary moments
in my ordinary text...

the story of this life of mine,
it's merit is but lame.
What have I
to boast
or feats to toast
in my ordinary shame?

I'm "just a" this, or "just a" that...
few letters follow my name.
So doldrums come,
steal over me,
as I've no stake to claim.

This world would leave me, outcast.
This world would let me roam.
This world would care not for my tears,
but...
this world is not my home.

I'm told You went to make a place,                    *John 14:2-3
a place for us, with You.                    *John 19:18, Galatians 3:13
I read You died a brutal death,                   *2 Corinthians 5:17
but rose to make me new.

So in this newness, cover me,
naked ambitions clothe...
tear my heart
til it's apart,
and break it
if it chose...

to honor other gods than You
in thought or act or deed;
and make the Bread of Life                    *John 6:35
consist of all
I am
to feed.

For what was Mary but a virgin?               *Luke 1:26-28
Or Adam but a man?                            *Genesis 1:26
And what was the mouth of Moses               *Exodus 3:10-12
apart from the Great I AM...?

Burning
in a bush;                                    *Exodus 3:1-10
Handwritten
on a wall;                                    *Daniel, Chapter 5
Thrown
from a whale:                                 *Jonah 2:1-10
and other tales
of those whom
You have called...

So send me, LORD, for here...                 *Isaiah 6:8
I am,
a sheep within Your fold!                     *John 10:14
Sear my lips and make them clean,
with blazing flame-dipped coal...             *Isaiah 6:6-7

and burn away my dross                        *Malachi 3:2-3
leaving my soul so scathed,
that I might someday
hope to have
*extra-ordinary* faith!

# OUR CLOUDED LOOKING GLASS

Corrupted man,
our human kind—
too sick at heart                                        *Jeremiah 17:9
to even mind

the cesspool of
our wanton cravings;
the nagging strife
with every raving.

Stricken by a venomous asp,                              *Genesis 3:1
we reach for footing—but cannot grasp

and drown, submerged, when bitter
reign
devours                                                  *1 Peter 5:8
and sours
our hunger pain...                                       *Matthew 5:6

til we ignore it
burden free;
but should abhor it                                      *Romans 12:9
violently:

this sin
we're in
through tainted eyes
that cannot see                                          *Matthew 13:14-15
what under,
lies...                                                  *John 8:44

to steal, kill, and destroy                              *John 10:9-10
the prodigal girls and boys;                             *Luke 15:11-32

so everything we touch is marred
and every word we speak has scarred.

The soul's a hollow, vacant cavity
filled only with total depravity.                    *Genesis 6:2-16

And in this trespass we are dead—                    *Ephesians 2:1-3
as grass that withers,                    *Isaiah 40:6-7, 1 Peter 1:24-25
save Words in Red!                    *Isaiah 40:8, Matthew 24:35

And with our sight restored from blind....                    *John 9:1-25
we ask, receive;
we seek, and find...                    *Matthew 7:7-8

and can't resist 'spite all defenses
this tender *Grace* beyond our senses...                    *1 Peter 5:10

that compels, commands, and calls
us to the writing on the wall.                    *Daniel, Chapter 5

So we will pray and persevere                    *Hebrews 10:36, James 1:2-3
knowing God's plan will come to pass;
for someday
we'll see the Way,                    *John 14:6
but for now...
our clouded looking glass.                    *1 Corinthians 13:12

# POUND OF CURE

Once upon a time,
there was a little child.
With big brown eyes
and sweet goodbyes,
his temper meek and mild.

But then a sickness
came and threatened
to take hold
of this sweet child's life,
his family, and his soul.

This ailment was severe,
and only blood could save.                    *Leviticus 17:11, Exodus 12:13,
                                                        Hebrews 9:22

And so, the good nurse
fought for it,
so that child
would know no grave.

And this was quite the struggle.
It caused them both much pain.
The child could scarcely comprehend
or see the point and gain.

It's like this when we wrestle,        *Genesis 32:22-32, Hosea 12:3-6
when we're in a cistern well.                    *Jeremiah 2:13
It's like this
when we question God
despite the fires of hell.

It's like this when fear
what we do not understand,
the times of grief and heartache
when cannot see His plan.

And, yes, the baby wiggled.
He wrenched and even screamed—
when he saw the needle
that to him only seemed...

to be a source of suffering,
a stinging, burning prick.
And he didn't want to face it;
didn't care if he was sick.

How often do we do this?
How seldom is our praise...
when in a circumstance
that causes doubts to raise?

How often do we neglect
a joyful noise in Sunday chorus,                    *Psalm 100:1-5
when at a wit's end because
a trial has been set before us?

It's good there is a loving God,
a Great Physician, wise—                              *Mark 2:17
who orders what we need
albeit blessings in disguise.

He ordains all of our suffering
for greater good designed;
when all we see are needles,
pain, and hands that hold to bind.

So next time trust is losing ground
and you do realize it,
be still and know                                     *Psalm 46:10
that faith will grow
each time you exercise it.          *Hebrews 12:1-3, 2 Peter 1:5-9

For without faith we can't please God,           *Hebrews 11:6
of this we can be sure...
and one ounce of prevention
will beat a pound of cure.

# PRAYER FOR REVIVAL

I know You from the days of old,                    *Hebrews 13:8
I know Your strength and Spirit, bold!

I know You though my struggles are
deep and high and wide and far.

I know that you have rescued me
with all your love on Calvary's Tree!        *Luke 23:33, John 19:17

But all I know is limited,                        *1 Corinthians 13:12
for You, oh LORD, are from some hid…              *Matthew 13:13

Your mysteries are yet unveiled
to children, meek, who've not withheld…              *Mark 10:15

their pride and ego - sweet life itself        *Matthew 16:25, Luke 9:24
praise and prayers, time and wealth -

yet through a clouded mirror see                  *1 Corinthians 13:12
we all your glory, truth and He…

Who gave His life and died for us,                    *Romans 5:8
for Whom we pine and witness much                      *Acts 1:8

Oh, give us strength to run this race -            *Hebrews 12:1-2
let sin not be our resting place!

But make us rise as old dry bones                  *Ezekiel 37:1-14
did in the valley from Your throne!

Ezekiel did prophesy,
and now I call on You, Most High!

Rain down your love and flood this earth,            *Hosea 6:1-3
awaken us in great rebirth!                        *Ephesians 5:14

Hide not Your face that shelters all,           *Psalm 27:9
but quench the thirst of righteous call...    *Matthew 5:6

with Your sweet water, living pure -        *John 4:14
and let our sickened hearts endure...    *Jeremiah 17:9

all shame for you and for your cross,
but let us bring Him to the lost!

Open their eyes, let their ears hear
that You are mighty, gracious, NEAR!      *Psalm 34:18

For them, I love, and them I pray—
let Your Strong Spirit lead the Way...      *John 14:6

that leads, though narrow, straight to life    *Matthew 7:14
and brings great joy among the strife!    *John 15:11

I know You from the days of old,
I'll know You til my blood runs cold...

for Your great grace and Kingdom's sake -
arise Your bride, may she *awake!*    *Ephesians 5:32; Romans 13:11

# PRAYER FOR THE BROKEN VESSEL

This vessel, meek and lowly,
one made for certain wrath...                    *Jeremiah 19:1-14
its parts in disarray
like a powered, scattered calf;                  *Exodus 32: 19-20

it's broken...
into pieces
so I cry to You, Most High                       *Psalm 91:1
I am
this shattered vessel
and at times I know not why

the marks that I keep missing,
the strife this causes – pain...
and yet I swear
I cannot help but
*fall*
into an old refrain

temptation is a monster
who hides
inside
the night
under my bed
from closets, fed,
it on my soul and might;

and yet I know You, God of mine,
I know You've led me to it...
this brink
this edge
this driving wedge
calling me
to suffer through it

as Job would face disaster                                     *Job 19:23-25
as Joseph, left for dead,
in cisterns deep                                          *Genesis 37:18-36
from troubled sleep
but faith, I keep, instead

as Isaac, waiting patiently,
as Rebekah herself was led...
'long camel trails,
her face in veils,
this longing bride to wed                                 *Genesis 24:62-67

as Paul wrote to the Romans
these things I hate, I do                                      *Romans 7:15
for all have erred                                            *Romans 3:23
like harlots wear
the scarlet, crimson hue

of a coward,
of unbelief,
of abominations – lies...
from murders
and immoral sex
from sorcery, idols, *cries*

a people and their conscious,
now seared in brazen sins
yet to the Way                                                  *John 14:6
we'll turn
again,
through belief that lends...

such gifts, so irrevocable!                                  *Romans 11:29
Can I question You exist?
When those You call,
to a Wailing Wall,
by grace none can resist!

So take these shattered pieces,
mold them again in time...
into a vessel fit for use                              *Romans 9:21-26
by inscribed hands, divine.                            *Isaiah 49:14-16

Yes, shape it by Your will
through great baptismal flame,                            *Matthew 3:11
so no thrown stone                                          *John 8:37
(or a harsh word)
can crack or dent its frame!

As Malachi's refining fire,                              *Malachi 3:1-3
or Nebuchadnezzar's rage,
in a furnace full of heat                                *Daniel 3:1-30
where sin might meet
its consequential wage.                                  *Romans 6:23

Then let it grow,
and glow and glow,
til strong enough to hold
a WELL of
        water
        turned to
        wine...                                            *John 2:1-11
for this daughter                                        *Zechariah 9:9
and Lamb once slaughtered                                *Isaiah 53:7
whose wedding supper finds...                            *Revelation 19:7

the blessed ones,
the chosen,
who walked and did not faint                             *Isaiah 40:31
who'll come to dine
in linen, fine,
as righteous acts of saints!                             *Revelation 19:8

This vessel, meek and lowly,
once made for certain wrath—
its pieces mend,
Almighty Friend,                                           *John 15:15
Who makes known the living path.                           *Psalm 16:11

# QUESTIONS OF THE HEART

Outside the pups were begging,        *Matthew 15:24-28
the housework's left undone...
cause all of me
falls to my knees
to seek        *Matthew 7:7-8
the Father's Son.        *John 10:30

I want to know what is my fate?
My path to take or leave?
I what to know what is my call--
from Him or my own needs?

I cannot know this heart of mine,
it's sick        *Jeremiah 17:9
and wanting more.
Are aspirations truly divine
or am I on a course...

of vain pursuit and agony,
for fame and riches—wealth?
I choose to ask the God Who
knows me better than myself.

For did not Judas betray our King
with just a tender kiss...?        *Luke 22:48
Could I not do the same
through vain ambition's
brooding wish...?

And did not Peter make the claim
that he was tried and true...?
But did not he deny the LORD
when asked if Christ, he knew...?    *Matthew 26:34, Mark 14:66-72

Then did not Thomas doubt                                    *John 20:24-29
His rising from a dark, cold tomb...?
Do I not now doubt His birthing
from within the reborn womb...?                              *John 3:1-3

Do I now doubt His power
to take a trembling,                                         *Philippians 2:12
fearing soul...?
Embolden it,
inmost being knit,                                           *Psalm 139:13-14
and for His Kingdom
give a role?

Do I not stammer as Moses,
seeing only my slow speech...?                               *Exodus 4:10
Do I not wait as Gideon
longing for a dew-filled fleece...?                          *Judges 6:33-40

But—
did the valley of old dry bones
not rise at God's command?                                   *Ezekiel 37:1-10
And were not the sticks of
Joseph and Ephraim
taken in the prophet's hand?                                 *Ezekiel 37:15-28

Did not the rocks and waves take form
from the breath of life God's spoken?                        *Genesis 1:1-10
Did not Joseph dream                                         *Genesis 37:5-7
and Rahab scheme                                             *Joshua 6:17
or from death sleepers have woke?                            *Mark 5:35-43

Like such, form me
that I might see                                             *Matthew 13:16
Your true and loving Way                                     *John 14:6
where grace abounds                                          *John 1:16
and
I am
found                                                        *Luke 15:1-10
so that Your wrath is stayed!

Now hungering pups
are satisfied,
all's clean,
and my soul's still.                    *Psalm 46:10
I know I am just
a piece of clay,                         *Isaiah 45:9
forming by the Potter's will.      *2 Corinthians 4:7

# ABRAHAM'S RAINBOW

I drove to the beach today.
It seemed a
waste of sunshine
not to go,
because it had been raining
so I hoped to see
a great rainbow.                                           *Genesis 9:13-16

There I spotted
a caramel-colored woman
with dark, almond-shaped eyes.
Her long hair reached
the small of her back
and is just as course and thick
as mine, but even at the ends
and coal black—darker than my own.
Two tiny crosses of silver
reflect the Son
in each of her ears.

Then I notice another lady
at the water's edge.
Her skin reminds me of
bitter-sweet dark chocolate.
She's wearing a one-piece swimsuit
with a marble gray-white pattern,
and her long, exotic braids
dance freely about her shoulders.
She's walking with a man
as dark as ebony.
From his broad shoulders
down to the middle of his being
sways a cross of gold
that's big enough to bear.
And he caught my cap

as it blew past
like any
Good Samaritan.                                        *Luke 10:25-37

One young girl
has coal black waves
that reach her elbows, and
the six-pointed
Star of David
dangles round
her dainty neck.

One guy is wearing
full-length camouflage trousers
but cannot hide
with his tattoos of all variety,
one of Christ's crucifixion.
(We bleed for what we love.)
His skin is alabaster
not white like a sheet...
but a ghost—*familiar*                                 *Acts 2:38
to me,
somehow.

My own skin is ivory,
but turning
into a painful pink.
Pain means change,                                     *Romans 5:3-5
and I should
no doubt
darken up in days
into a healthy tan
like my grandpa had.
His skin was olive
and of Cheyenne descent...
though my grandma's name
was Patterson,
and she had

green Irish eyes
that read the Bible
to me
from a rocking chair.

But now all of us
have converged
at the edge
of the water today.

Some jump in headlong,
while others wade a while.

I step gradually,
waiting for each
impending wave.

But a lukewarm splash
just *sickens* me,                                        *Revelation 3:16
so I head further out—
I want to roll
with bigger waves.
They come in high and hard.
But that gets boring fast,
because the water is so soft,
moving through me,
so I wait for the next big wave…
and when it comes
I float freely
on top of its crest.
And after that I soon felt
the safe floor of wet sand
beneath my feet.

Craving yet more excitement,
I throw myself into
the next wave
and it slaps my torso. Undaunted,

I run faster into the next,
defiant—over confident.
And this next wave was bigger
than I'd intended.
It grabbed my tip toes
out from under me
and its crest lapped
over my head,
left my frail pail body
helpless under
its mounting weight,
and my mouth left
gaping out of breath
and underwater...
being thrown back like
*a fisherman's reject,*                              *Matthew 4:19
tossed roughly
but safely against the shore
with a vicious case of sand-burn
and
the sickly tart taste
from the
salt of the earth                                    *Matthew 5:13-16
and the sea
in my throat.

Still...I went back again,
humbled,                                             *Proverbs 3:34
just content to float
for a bit
atop the waves.

Despite my obvious
failure at sea
*I knew*
my Older Brother                                     *Hebrews 2:1
Who has gone before
-further out-

into the *deep*                                    *Luke 5:4, John 21:6
and was there to save me,                              *Luke 9:56
could
walk on water                                      *Matthew 14:25
if He chose to.

So I just HAD to get this right,
I spot another roller coaster wave
and let it consume me,
fell helpless backward with it,
let it wash me,                                        *Romans 6:4
held my breath
as it pulled me under,
ignoring the stinging stench
of salt water sneaking
into my left nostril
and the burning in my lungs.

For that one moment
I felt as one
with the ocean
and nature,
in submission to it all                                *James 4:7
and God Himself,
until the wave
sat me
on the shore
to see
around some more.

Happy-go-lucky people
by the thousands now
were still
clustered all around
at hot dog stands
on roller blades
and bikes cycling,
weaving smoothly

in and out
just like the waves
that move the wading masses.
I hated to leave
this unique paradise.

Sadly, I noticed that the sky
had offered no rainbow,
but I couldn't be disappointed
with so many multi-colored
umbrella tops bowed up
to stake out
billions of different little
claims and cultures...
God's *promise*,                     *Genesis 22:15-18, Hebrews 6:13-15
after all.

Author's Note:
I know what you're thinking, it was Noah whose story involved a
rainbow! But so was Abraham's story, in a manner of speaking. You
see, he was promised descendants as numerous as the stars of the
skies and the sands of the oceans!

# RAIN TREE SPOTTING

We ride along the road,
and she points out a tree                                        *Psalm 1:3
with light pink patches blooming,
lovely, for all the world to see.                            *Matthew 13:16

She tells me, "It's a rain tree."
And we ride further on
in hopes to spot another
with light pink patches donned.

She's been around for quite a while,
with wisdom like a jewel;                                    *Proverbs 8:11
she carries herself with dignity,
living by the golden rule.                                      *Luke 6:31

Her hands are aged with time
and reach out to embrace
just any passer by
who eyes
her warm and smiling face.

And she's not one for discourse
on politics that divide,
and when pinned to answer says
she'll not take any side.

She rather looks for
what is pure
and the noblest of things,                             *Philippians 4:8
and gives praise
so spirits raise
in joyful noises to our King.                                *Psalm 98:4

She inspires me to be better
in my love for fellow man;

there is a Light within her
that's been put up on a stand.                          *Matthew 5:14-16


She's really like the rain tree
who stands through
weather cold or warm—
with light pink patches, perfect,
in their poise and stately charm.


This tree                                              *Galatians 3:13
she sees,                                              *Matthew 13:16
it comforts me—
reminds me of a better place                              *John 14:2-3
where God will hold us near;                               *James 4:8
wipe every tear;                                        *Revelation 21:4
and reign in almighty grace.


Oh let us be like rain tree, LORD,
who flourish along the Way...                              *Acts 22:4
to bless the scene
in peace, serene,
growing for You come what may.


Yes, let us be like her, dear God,
whose womb was never barren...
but fertile like fields
who ever yield
the blessed Rose of Sharon.                          *Song of Songs 2:1

Author's Note:
While serving as a caregiver for a home health agency, I had a
privilege of working with an older lady who inspired this poem. She
was the epitome of faith and grace. And she was madly in love with
Jesus. I often thought that she was who I want to be when I grow up.
And in our drives on errands, she would point out each and every
Raintree. To me, her gentle nature came to symbolize the bride of
Christ, the church herself. And so I penned this poem one day in
her honor. She has since gone on to be the LORD to Whom she was
so very faithful. And I dare say, this world has lost a saint.

# REMEMBERING GRACE

With every fallen word,
and every verse misheard,
I'm reminded of sin
that wins again
when it's what I have preferred.

With every vile slip of the tongue
and vanities                                        *Ecclesiastes 1:1-2
on which I've hung
all plans and dreams,
conniving schemes,
I'm reminded of sin
that wins again
with empty praises sung.

With every enemy I have not loved              *Matthew 5:43-48
or stranger I have refused,                     *Matthew 25:31-46
with every pride                                  *Proverbs 16:18
I've idolized,
and monies I've misused…
I'm reminded of sin
that wins again
over this weak reed, unbruised.                      *Isaiah 42:3

And so where is my hope,
in this, my sin-stained fate?
And will I ever learn
or dare to turn
from profane acts and hate?

How long am I to bear
such an anxious load?
How long must I endure?
Or is there a cure
along this broken road…?                             *Isaiah 45:2

That leads me to its end
when on a cross
*I see:*                                                *Matthew 13:16
these sins of mine
through hands, divine,
that are driven in a tree.                              *Galatians 3:13

And on it hangs my *Hope,*                              *Psalm 119:114
for on it is the Way                                       *John 14:6
that I'm redeemed
from all which seems
to make me want to stray!

So to there, I'll look
and to there, I'll turn
my newfound smiling face,
undaunted by sin
that will loose by then
to Christ's sweet, saving grace.                        *Hebrews 4:16

# REVELATIONS NEAR MIDNIGHT

imagined importance
in emerald-studded everythings
our world                                          *James 4:4
a tiny scope—the centromere
of wanton emotions
and frivolous things
like so many dominoes
-like people and
the games they play-
inside gated lives
so rich with boundaries,
caged in
illusive empires
afforded for
all eyes to see
(but do not see)                              *Matthew 13:14-15
and to shed light
from a luciferin source                    *2 Corinthians 11:14
dimly lit
by blue-green chandelier tip
reflections,
flickering (snickering)
but bright enough
to attract
like aurora borealis
beckoning
a writhing sea
into the dark and cold
unknown, unfamiliar channels, an abyss
so hollow, void like
contracts signed
on dotted lines
and sold
in the nick of time
as waves roll overhead

submerging
-in too deep-
completely WASHED
and yet unclean
guided by an age-old
lucid arch angel                               *Isaiah 14:12-14, Luke 10:18
that drifts among us
seamlessly
through crimson and lavender oils
so refined,
above reproach
are these horrible things
let to stand
inside the temple
where incantation
smoke is blown
incensed
to hypnotize
the wading masses
of devout followers,
undaunted despite
Truth                                           *John 14:6
and heirs to the
Kingdom of Heaven
who cry out
with no one to suffer them
or rival perceived authority
not to mention
bloody clinic floors
and battlefields of
no less consequence
these
reigning cats and dogs
will have their moment
in the limelight

...quite apart
from the Son...

with no mortal wind
strong enough to
sweep away the
wicked witches
of the east
or the west
where forest fires devour
and mud slides sour, sloping
downward into homelessness
and diseased apathy of
laissez-faire campaigns
that got US over a barrel
of crude complaints
and black sheep's wool
pulled over eyes
already blind,
lost
and lacking
any focus…

…how I welcome baptismal floods
of Living Water                              *John 7:38
in a deluge bursting free
from all the damned and disenchanted,
ripping through
our stony fortress, leaving no one
left
to lie.

# RICH CRIMSON RAN

Rich crimson ran
into a tree,                                        *Galatians 3:13
staining it,
for you and me.

It was a sight,
so sore to be
lift up                              *Numbers 21:9, John 3:14-15
for one and all
to see.                                            *Matthew 13:16

Rich crimson ran
to wash me white.                                    *Psalm 51:7
I am
made whole,                                        *Mark 5:25-34
from blind to sight...                              *John 9:1-25

of this fiery serpent's pole
where rich crimson ran
to save my soul!                                   *Romans 1:16

# ROCK IN A RAVINE

My wayward soul,
so prone to stray,
has lost its sight...                                    *Proverbs 3:21
and I, my Way.                              *John 14:6, Acts 19:9

Desensitized to
sin and shame—
so full of pride, I talk on;                        *Proverbs 16:18
but I'm surrounded
by my pain and
water I can't walk on.                         *Matthew 14:22-23

And in its torrent,
stealing joy,                                       *John 10:9-10
this current's so dark and seething.
It snatches me
along its path, so fierce,
that I'm left                                  *Matthew 24:40-41
barely breathing.

It smothers me
within its vice,
I'm drowning by its weight.
I'm tossed about by every wave        *Ephesians 4:14, James 1:6
within this vengeful strait.

Ensnared by it,
I funnel down
this raging cold ravine...
begging only
my LORD save me,                               *Matthew 1:21
that He come to intervene.

Helpless there,
I cast my care,                                        *1 Peter 5:7
and pray for Christ's firm hand,
knowing He                                             *John 17:3
Who calms the sea        *Matthew 8, Mark 4:35-41, Luke 8:22-25
is my Rock on which to stand!        *Isaiah 28:16, Matthew 7:24-27

# SEAFARER'S PRAYER

At times when winds beat down on me
and all hope turns to dread
with my little boat
scarcely afloat
and crests towering overhead...

I will remember You are the one
Who soothes the striving sea;          *Matthew 8:23-27, Mark 4:35-41
commanding to be still                                    *Psalm 46:10
all at Your will
'til raging thunders cease.

And, so in my calamity
when I'm not in control...
wake from the stern,
quiet waves that churn
and threaten to take hold.

Because this whirlwind does not own me!
It cannot drown my plea!
And no gale or gust                              *Romans 8:38-39
can sway my trust...
for You calm the storm in me.

# SEED OF CHRIST

Seed of Christ...
that fell in me,
my shallow soil –                                       *Matthew 13:5
how can it be?

Seed of Christ...
how can you stay
in such a broken
vessel's clay?                                          *2 Corinthians 4:7

Seed of Christ...
did not the birds
yet come to snatch                                      *Matthew 13:4
Your perfect words?

Seed of Christ...
I pray you grow,                                        *Matthew 13:8
so I might reap                                         *Galatians 6:7-9
good that I sow

Seed of Christ...
don't let the sun                                       *Matthew 13:6
scorch tender leaves
til they're undone

Seed of Christ...
don't let thorns choke                                  *Matthew 13:7
Your burdens light
and easy yoke                                           *Matthew 11:28-30

Seed of Christ...
be deeply rooted;
Your word not wither,
or be convoluted

Seed of Christ...
that brings rebirth,                          *John 3:1-3
spring up in me
'spite stony earth!

Seed of Christ...
come blossom through
my pain and suffering
like spring, renewed!

And break this ground
for harvest fields,                          *Luke 10:2
Sweet Seed of Christ...
that fruit, it yields!                       *Galatians 5:22-23

# SEEDS FOR THOSE IN NEED

Some people's days
are strung like pearls
on silken, blissful strings—
but our's seem
nailed together
in hap-hazard broken rings...

...like the circle of a hamster's wheel,
we run and spin and toil,
-going nowhere-
while filth piles up and tempers boil.

Our house is dark and ugly.
No one wants inside.
        And so we sit
        alone in it,
as all the days go by.

Outside the truck
is broken down,
        the engine doesn't run.
Now the dryer's busted,
and wet clothes
        are left undone.

The tv's out of order;
the channels don't come in.
And electric heaters hiss
while glowing evil grins.

Will this be our fate forever,
are we confined to die...
in this dreary aftermath
of mistakes made by and by?

Should we sit
and lie
in this,
accept our lot in life?
Is there no way out
from such torment
and such strife?

What hope
is there when joy
is buried below
our circumstances?
Can we rise above the waves
*someday*
and live to takes our chances?

When Israelites felt
left to die
in one place or another,
some chose to follow
God's command                                   *Joshua, Chapter 2
as opposed to being smothered...

...in a desert wasteland
that consumed a generation,                      *Numbers 14:20-24
as now
the enemy roams about                                  *1 Peter 5:8
and pines for our damnation.

So many mountains
left to move...
and all we have, indeed,
is a tiny bit of faith
just like a mustard seed.                         *Matthew 17:20

But...
as Jael took up
her hammer
and drove the tent steak down;                    *Judges 4:16-24
as Deborah rode in victory                        *Judges, Chapter 5
singing a song, renowned;

as Ester risked
her life for Jews
whom she did cherish...
sending word to Mordecai,
that if she would perish, she'd perish;               *Ester 4:16

as Joshua cried
the sun stood still                                *Joshua 10:11-14
that moon gave way and stopped...
for battle neath
a blazing sky,
for faith that would not drop;

as David penned
so many Psalms,
as Moses raised his staff...                        *Exodus 14:16
as God the Father
will separate true grain
from the chaff.                              *Matthew 3:12, Luke 3:17

For
I AM                                          *Exodus 3:14, Mark 14:62
promised
nothing more
than a cross,
its weight to bear...                            *Matthew 16:24-26
as all of these
I hope to please
only Christ,
for Whom I care.

And so in loss and poverty
I mourn                                                *Matthew 5:4
this broken spirit's state—
that I would want
more than I'm entitled,
want more than what His fate...

has dealt me now
in sadness, grief—
my idle-minded pity...
draws me astray
from the only Way                                      *John 14:6
I will become a shining city...                        *Matthew 5:14

perched on hill
for all to see,                                        *Matthew 13:16
Light of the World                                     *John 8:12
to know...
that God in Heaven
still longs for us—
as ages past, ago!

That suffering produces perseverance,
that character fosters hope;                           *Romans 5:3-5
that we are
set apart
by grace with which to cope.                           *John 1:16

And so in hardships
let me lean
on these who've gone before,
their passion and their virtues
from faith that was restored.

Let many trees
be born of me
from my sowing the smallest seeds...                    *Matthew 13:31-32
some hundred-fold,
some thousand-fold,
some millions more to feed!

I am relieved
for Christ believes
His seeds
are all we need.

# SEPARATED

When I am separated
from God's Presence and His will,
there is a hollow tomb in me
I cannot rightly fill.

When I am separated
from God's Spirit and His Way;                    *John 14:6, Acts 19:9
there lurks a darkened fog,
causing me to go astray.

When I am separated
from God altogether—torn apart,
there towers
a brooding hedge
surrounding my cold heart.

When there's more of me
and less of Christ—
then sin is let to reign,
and a bitter hatred seethes in me
that no one can restrain.

Though loose to roam,
do as I please—
a rage in me remains;
so no true freedom
breathes in me.
I'm bound by crippling chains...                    *John 8:34

until I seek the Son                                *John 10:30
who shines through
all of my mournful groans                    *Matthew 5:4, Romans 8:26
I draw near,                                            *James 4:8
to Christ and hear                                 *Matthew 13:16
His Words                                          *Matthew 24:35
from Heaven's Throne.

# SHADOW DANCER

A waif gray image
that's caught a ride,
and follows after—
but has to hide,

having no real life
of its own
content to race
around unknown.

Chasing after any man
depending on...
      where he stands:

in the Light                                    *John 8:12
or shady play,
in the street
or in the Way.                                  *John 14:6

For in the Light
it can't be found,
but let Light fade
and it abounds.

The shadow dancer
scampers round—
seeking what
it hasn't found...

through wayward gates,
open and flirtin'
where nothing's long
and nothing's certain.

Getting bounced
'gainst walls or tossed,
across the ground
and often lost.

Appearing again
from nowhere to stand,
"Jump, fetch, or sit..."
on some command.

But shadows really
deserve much more—
to become real,
and holy adored.

So what then would
that dancer be
part from the chase
of feet and knees?
What could
sustain her
so fully...
but the *salvation*
of being free?                    *John 8:31-32

                                  *Genesis 2:18
God made woman
from and for
a man's side...                   *Genesis 2:22-23
not from some shadow
that's *cast aside*.

# SHIPWRECKED

The storm is here
and closing in...
So oft' I ask -
was it my sin...

that caused the waves
to lap o'er head?
And winds to beat                                        *Matthew 7:25
so much I dread...

another breath, another day,
another time that I might stay—

confined within this cell to die
until I call on the Most High!                           *Psalm 91:1

Who comes to me as gentle Brother,        *Hebrews 2:11-12
instills in me to love none other      *Exodus 20:3, Deuteronomy 6:5

than Him first, the Triune Spirit;
that storms, He calms—                         *Matthew 8:23-27,
no need to fear it!

For every curse, He's there to break;         *Exodus 20:5-6
for every hurt, and each mistake...

He quiets the wind—says to be still,            *Psalm 46:10
and waves to cease all at His will.

I know my God, my refuge strong!                *Psalm 46:1
I cling to Him, 'mid every song...

and joyful noise that 'scapes my lips...        *Psalm 98:4
'spite stormy seas and desperate ships.

# SILENCE SETS APART

What do I do with silence?
with stillness in the morn?
When there's no bussle,
or frantic hussle,
to get people out the door?

What do I do with stillness,
when the angst in me is stirred?
What do I do with silence,
that speaks louder than my words?

What do I do with Calm,
as He stares me in the face?
What do I do, knowing...
I have sinned against His grace?

What do I do with hardship?
With vanity? With despair?
But call God's name,
lighting a flame                           *Hebrews 12:29
to burn such casted cares.        *Psalm 55:22, 1 Peter 5:7

Yes, burn away what hinders me,
that keeps me so impure,
and hold me in the fire with You
so that I may endure.

Refining Fire,                                *Malachi 3:2-3
blaze in me...
for all You suffered on that tree,        *Galatians 3:13
and cremate all the dross.
Yes, come and sear
sins I hold dear.
Let me take up my cross!              *Matthew 16:24-26

So that when silence falls on me
and stillness cloaks my heart
I'll be at peace                                          *Philippians 4:6
with striving ceased
and truly set apart.
Sons of Shame

*Mephibosheth,*                                    *2 Samuel, Chapter 9
of broken frame,
there is no honor
in your name!

A father killed,
and legs now lame -
a curse from which
you must have came...

or so was feared
by one and all,
when young King David
came to call...

and seek you out
on whom to pour
God's sweet love
& blessings more!

From brokenness you did ascend
on eagle's wings,                                          *Isaiah 40:31
pure as the wind                                             *John 3:8

that blew you back to life again
from a dead dog to man and then                    *2 Samuel 9:8

you sat within sweet cedar walls,
as distinguished heir of Saul!                          *2 Samuel 9:9

And like him yet
we all will be
for those partaking
of the Tree…                                        *Revelation 2:7

of Life, in death
there is no hold -
that can
withstand...
this truth be told!

From mouths of babes
and prophets old,
lame legs will run
on streets of gold!                                *Revelation 21:21

Blind eyes will see
deaf ears will hear                                 *Isaiah 35:5
the glory of
the One so near...

transform us now!
From teeth that gnash -
give us Your beauty
from the ash.…                                      *Isaiah 61:3

of dusty roads and dying towns
of rivers dry,
where thirst abounds                               *Matthew 5:6

where we hunger
for all, but Bread                                  *John 6:35
where our souls
are lost and often led

out into all that's vanity                         *Ecclesiastes 1:2
depriving us of sanity...

as we stumble day by day,
loosing sight of His Sweet Way.                    *John 14:6

Oh, call us back from unseen danger!
Let us not answer to a stranger!                    *John 10:5

As sheep before a Shepherd bleat
we cast our crowns now at Your feet.          *Revelation 4:10

Lend a smooth white stone                          *Revelation 2:17
and a new name,
so we're no longer
sons of shame.

# SPARK OF FAITH

a stack of bills
too high to pay…
a diagnosis
that came today…

a wayward child,
a bankruptcy…
a devastation
none could foresee…

a job that's lost,
an aching need…
a longing pang
that none can feed…

I look to God
within His Word—
    to see                               *Matthew 13:16
    I'm not the first
of all His children suffering;
of those who've had it worse.

I see…
    Joseph in a cistern;                *Genesis 37:12-36
    and Jonah in a whale.               *Jonah 2:1-10
I see…
    Paul endure the shipwrecks     *Acts, Chapters 27-28
    from the sea's steep churning gale.

I see…
    Lot flee Gomorrah;                *Genesis 19:1-29
I see…
    David honor Saul.                *1 Samuel 26:10-11
I see…
    the tears of Peter

at the rooster's third
stark scolding call.                                   *Luke 22:54-62

I see...
        Mephibosheth
        seated at the King's good table;        *2 Samuel, Chapter 9
I see...
        Noah's ark;                              *Genesis, Chapters 6-7
        burning bush's spark;                         *Exodus 3:1-3
        Mary birthing in a stable.                      *Luke 2:1-21

So seeing these
who've gone before—
whose faith I scarcely comprehend...
I am
ashamed
to call the name
of the Master Who calls me, "Friend."                   *John 15:15

For what is all my suffering worth,
if not to bring God glory?
Just pain alone
upon the throne
of self-pity's grousing story.

So let me suffer
for His namesake—                                     *Matthew 5:11
let me not miss the mark;
let me show that pain
is not in vain
when faith sustains
us through the dark...

just like a lighted flame
that none of us should hide,
but place onto a candlestick
shedding light
to all inside!                                        *Matthew 5:15

# SUNSHINE AND THE RAIN

Rain falls on us
out of the sky
it comes with raging wind.
And we can't control
as heat takes its toll
from sunshine now and then.

We question,
why the damp?
And why the scorching rays?
Such two extremes
to us, it seems,
we have seen better days.

But did we think,
perhaps forget...
that plants
need both to thrive?
Sometimes it's easy
in our haste
to curse in battle cries...

our cold wet socks
and circumstance,
a sunburn's dark crisp sting...
the consequence of
getting drenched
or burned
within hellacious rings

through which we have to jump
at times
to gain a living wage,
out into the weather
trudging toward another age

in which we hope
for ways to cope,
pining for a lighter load…
with not a care
or cross to bear                              *Matthew 16:24-26, Luke 9:23
on a still not taken road.

What is this curse?                    *Exodus 20:4-5, Deuteronomy 5:9-10
The fall of all—                                          *Genesis 3:1-17
the age old Sunday story…
our God ordained
suffering
s'posed to bring Him
so much glory…?

to toil the earth,                                          *Genesis 3:17
and find rebirth                                            *John 3:1-3
through a Way that is so narrow…                           *Matthew 7:14
which some despise
as a needle's eye                                         *Matthew 19:24
tells vultures from the sparrow

who falls                                                *Matthew 10:29
as Eve,                                                   *Genesis 3:16
but still conceives
the message, Man, and might
of our Triune God
Whose wrath                              *Proverbs 3:11, Hebrews 12:5-6
and rod                                                   *Psalm 23:4
brings both comfort
and due fright.                                           *Proverbs 9:10

He sends the rain
the aching cold
the flames of sun rays down                               *Matthew 5:45
upon His people
of the steeple
into a craving ground

that feeds
the seeds                                          *Matthew 13:1-8
which we all need
to grow
      a harvest so renowned...              *Revelation 14:15
and we will know
Him through His Word                               *2 Timothy 3:16
      despite our smiles or frowns.

He allows discomfort,
pleasure coupled with our pain;                  *1 Peter 4:19; 5:10
but best to worship the God Who's real
than idol ones in vain...                             *Exodus 20:2-6

the ones who tell us all is well,                      *Jeremiah 6:14
the ones who never mention hell;                  *Revelation 20:10

the ones who promise fortune – fame,
for believing in Christ's holy name;         *Matthew 6:24; 19:16-28

the ones who sin
      and *pride* in it,                                *Proverbs 16:18
the ones who *hate*                                  *1 John 3:15
      and side in it.

Though we might curse
or think Him worse
      than gods of lessor fame,
Yahweh provides it all
from deliverance to the fall;
      and for that, I'm not ashamed.              *Romans 1:16

# SWEET BALM OF GILEAD

There is a Balm in Gilead,                          *Jeremiah 8:22
Its fragrance sweet...
so it's been said.

There is a Balm in Gilead,
Its bark is dark...
Its flowers, *red*.

There is a Balm
with a costly toll—                          *1 Corinthians 6:19-20
our soul It takes
but saves our souls...                          *Acts 4:11-12

from the eternal second death,                  *Revelation 20:14
what sorrows                                 *2 Corinthians 7:10
bring in Baby's breath...                          *John 3:1-3

that grip us, haunt us, night and day
as we toil, and pine, and pray –
but rest assured, He's made a Way                  *John 14:6
for His impending Judgment Day!               *Revelation 20:13

There is a Balm in Gilead
as wand-like branches reach out to spread...

Good News about His soon return,
to one and all whose healing yearns...          *Revelation 22:2

for a great faith that makes them whole,          *Mark 5:34
it's Christ Who plays the central role!

He is the Balm of Gilead,
make Him your treasure first instead...          *Matthew 13:44-45

and feel the joy, the great relief               *John 15:11
from all you suffer - even grief!

He is the Balm of Gilead—
Who calms the sea!          *Matthew 8:23-27, Mark 4:35-41,
                                Luke 8:22-25
Who wakes the dead!         *Mark 5:35-42, John 11:43-44

"Come!" He calls, as trumpets blast…     *1 Corinthians 15:52
as heavens burst open at last.

Come to the Balm of Gilead--
for tears that Jeremiah shed.        *Jeremiah 8:18-21; 31:16-17

# SWEET GLIMPSE OF GRACE

I stand before the cross
and scarcely lift my chin;
because to face
such awesome grace—
I scarce can take it in.

For I have been unfaithful                          *Romans 3:23
and I have been untrue.
Like Paul,
I call
and cry for all
that which "I hate, I do."                          *Romans 7:15-20

Yes, I have sinned in anger,                        *Ephesians 4:26
and I am again ashamed…
whether in road rage;
poor steward of wage;                               *1 Corinthians 4:2
I'm the one deserving blame.

Yes, all of God's commandments
I've broken in my haste:
idolatry;                                           *Exodus 20:3
frivolity;
gluttony to the point of waste.                     *Proverbs 3:21

It haunts me now
as I do tremble,                                    *Philippians 2:12
mourning in the pew;
praying God can still forgive these sins.
praying I'll still be of the few…                   *Matthew 7:14

who are said to walk the narrow Way      *John 14:6, Acts 19:9
and find the Gate so small!                      *John 10:9-16
How far from me
this Gate must be,
as a child of Adam's fall.                          *Romans 5:12

What right have I
to raise my eyes
toward the cross I did not have to bear?
Yet I must see                          *Matthew 13:16
sin on that tree,                       *Galatians 3:13
knowing mine had put God there.

This blameless Lamb          *John 1:29, Revelation 5:12
atoning me,                             *1 John 2:1-2
so bludgeoned, scarred, and cursed—
what right have I
when I should die?                      *Ephesians 2:1-3
What sick ego's left to nurse?

So I will stand before the cross—
now humbly lift my chin;
with mercy new                      *Lamentations 3:22-23
each day
for few,
like me,
I'll run this race again...             *Hebrews 12:1-3

knowing that this is a covenant made for us,      *Luke 22:20
a new birth-right,                          *John 3:1-3
highly priced;                        *Matthew 13:44-45
in Whom I'm justified,                    *Romans 3:24-26
and slowly sanctified.              *2 Thessalonians 2:13
What sweet glimpse of grace
I see                                   *Matthew 13:16
in Jesus Christ!

# THANK GOD

We often thank God for pleasantries:
job promotions when all's at ease.
We often thank God entering His courts          *Psalm 100:4
when times are good with praise reports.

We often thank God when there's news
of weather fair, nothing to rue.

But do we thank God
when we are strained...?
when we are humbled,
finances drained...?

when clouds descend
with bitter rain...?
when peace is
harder to maintain...?

We thank God in the riches,
when stocks are high in worth.
We thank God in newest of spring,
when all the earth's at birth.

But in poverty and wanton need,
where is our gratitude...
for times that bring us to our knees,
so God can change our attitude?

We thank God in good health
when loved ones are well.
We thank God for that recovery
with praise reports to tell.

But in sickness and in death,
where is our thanks and praise...

that God deserves
for all our nerve
to doubt His higher ways?                                    *Isaiah 55:8-9

We thank God in the day,
but question Him at night...
even though we're told
that it's our role
to walk by faith, not sight.                               *2 Corinthians 5:7

And through it all God loves us still,
with mercies ever new...                             *Lamentations 3:22-23
setting apart
stony sick hearts                        *Ezekiel 36:25, Jeremiah 17:9
belonging to His few.                                       *Matthew 7:14

So don't pray for circumstances
when the soul is what's more dire.
Don't concentrate on problems
instead of sins
that send
us to the lake of fire.                                     *Revelation 20:10

Pray for wisdom, pray for peace
in all He brings your way.
Rest in His hands,
obey commands,
and there you'll ever stay.                                   *John 10:28

Thank God in the sunshine,
but also in the rain.                                        *Matthew 5:45
Thank Him for weather fare
and dare
to thank Him in our pain.

Thank God for being first;
thank Him for being last.                                   *Revelation 1:8
Thank God for hopeful futures

and for tragedies in the past.

Thank Him for green pastures
and still waters by our side.                    *Psalm 23:2
Thank Him for discipline                          *Job 5:17-18
on narrow paths that are not wide.          *Matthew 7:14

Thank Him for restoration
of our souls upon His breath.                   *Ezekiel 37:5
Thank Him for life He gives us
and for His timing in our deaths.           *Revelation 1:18

Be comforted within His will.
Do not despise His rod.                        *Proverbs 3:11-12
Persevere,                                          *James 1:12
          and let Him hear,
"Thank You, God, for being God."

# THANKS LIVING

Up and out of bed,
on the wrong side-
cursing work, but
having a way to provide.

Hating to cook;
avoiding the mess-
but knowing my children
are full is the best.

Fearing the doctor,
dreading his call-
but now closer to God
on my knees I will fall.

I will enter His courts                                            *Psalm 100:4
with thanks living today!
I'll rejoice in His praise
knowing He's made a way...                                        *John 14:6

for my sin to be final
and over and gone
with God's mercy new up
on each and every morn!                           *Lamentations 3:22-23

Suffering the cold,
but enjoying the snow!
Dampened by rain,
but I'll see its curved bow!                                    *Genesis 9:13

Sweltering in heat,
but warmed by the sun!
Broken by loss, but once
held my loved ones!

I will enter His courts                                        *Psalm 100:4
with thanks living today!
I'll rejoice in His praise
knowing He's made a way...                                     *John 14:6

for my sin to be final
and over and gone
with God's mercy new up
on each and every morn!                              *Lamentations 3:22-23

Sifting spittle with mud,
but to give sight to blind;                                    *John 9:6
trickling sweat with His blood,                               *Luke 22:44
but to leave death behind.                          *1 Corinthians 15:55-57

Turning tables in rage,                                    *Matthew 21:12
but to revel in truth;
choosing faith like a sage,
following God just as Ruth.                                   *Ruth 1:16-17

For the joy set before Him,
but grieving His loss;
despising its shame,
but enduring the cross!                                      *Hebrews 12:2

I will enter His courts                                      *Psalm 100:4
with thanks living today!
I'll rejoice in His praise
knowing He's made a way...                                     *John 14:6

for my sin to be final
and over and gone
with God's mercy new up
on each and every morn!                              *Lamentations 3:22-23

# THE BIBLE SITS BESIDE ME

I start another day
–all frantic, rushed, and hurried—
consumed by grief
with no relief
over things that have me worried.

The Bible sits beside me.
I move it out of the way.
I tell myself, "I'll get to it.
I've such a busy day."

But time just never comes,
and peace is not my friend;
as I bark at strangers driving
behind the wheel of all my sin.

A Bible's in the console.
It rides with me around.
But I've no chance to open it,
running errands through the town.

Home again, but can't relax.
The chores won't do themselves.
And Family Bibles, closed and quiet,
remain on dusty shelves.

Then tragedy strikes
and I am spent,
a mess from daily grinds.
"Where is God?! Doesn't He care?!"
I sputter and I whine.

Soon night falls down,
as what I've sown – I reap.
And my Bible rests

up on my chest,
but now I fall asleep.                                        *Revelation 3:2-3

Will God draw near                                                  *James 4:8
when we won't hear?                                           *Matthew 13:15
Will the Gardener                                               *John 20:11-18
plant a seed                                                    *Matthew 13:1-8
for fruit to yield                                                 *John 15:5
from a barren field                                           *Hebrews 6:1-8
that we don't tend or keep...?

Or will a Carpenter                                                *Mark 6:3
build a home
with foundation in loose sand;                            *Matthew 7:24-27
from wood and stone                                      *Deuteronomy 4:28
and that alone,
and expect it to withstand...

rain that falls and floods that come
and winds that fiercely blow...?
How can we presume to love a God—
one Whom we do not know?

The Bible just sat beside me,
until I knew its Poet.
For when I read
what God has said,
salvation's what I owe it!

# THE BRINK

Tossed at sea,
this rocky boat,
it cracks against the wind...                          *John 3:8
and waves do bear
but do not dare
pray for storms to rescind.

For I am lost
on maiden voyage
with weather less than fair...
and out of hope
when a noose's rope
brings comfort, not despair.

For at any time
I could end it,
and knowing that's control...
or so I think
I'd rather sink
than let fate take its toll

on what's left of sanity,
my body's aging state—
should I fear
an end is near
when all I've had, to date...

is misery
and heartache—
how much can a person take?
When grief looms
like some drizzly fog
round all my past mistakes.

I gasp for breath,
feel close to death,
and stumbling                                    *Matthew 18:7-10
          in my gait;
for this albatross
of pain and loss,
I smother neath its weight.

What have I done?
Was it Too much? Or simply not enough?
Of everything
and nothing
that's seemed to call a serpent's bluff.          *Job 1:11

Am I a pawn
moved cross a lawn
of checkered celestial game?
And should I be
on bended knee,
or curse God and die—in shame?                   *Job 2:9

So many questions
posed to me
and I cannot begin
to discern
-their answers, learn-
and choose not to pretend...

that I am more than dust and rib,               *Genesis 22:2
a worm despised by men,                          *Psalm 22:6
a donkey given speech                      *Numbers 22:22-35
that I might turn this path from sin.

And so no time for pity
and no time for wailing cries.
No time for anything
but finding blessings in disguise.

For from the dark
of a long ark                                    *Genesis 8:11
an olive Branch                                  *Jeremiah 33:15
did surrender…
its leaf to the Dove
of grace and love
sustaining hope so tender:

for a lost world's
New Covenant
that was bowed up in the sky,                    *Genesis 9:13-16
raised up in all its glory—
like the One Who came to die.        *Numbers 21:9, John 3:14-16

And when I see
the faith in Hebrews,                            *Hebrews, Chapter 11
of those who've gone before…
I question mine,
examine it,                                      *2nd Corinthians 13:5
knowing that I'll need much more.

But how can I attain it,
and where will it reside,
in a heart so dark
and jaded
like a stone that's cast aside?

So take all that is in me
when doubt creeps up in the night;
and dross, do purge
-let faith emerge-
and bless me in Your sight…

for I'm weak, as grains of sand,
that beg of some great ocean
to be washed
despite the cost
and all of my emotion.

Now strike the colors
of my mast—
in here, this lonely vessel
and set apart
this wayward heart                                    *Ezekiel 36:26
with whom God, alone, might wrestle.          *Genesis 32:26

# THE CALLING

What drives me to this cave of mine...?
This place to hide and wail...?
'Bout everything & nothing...
fear of chaos, fear I'll fail.

Sometimes I fear for my own soul.                    *Philippians 2:12
I fear I'm nothing more...
than all that I have come from,
generations past galore.                              *1 Kings 19:4

Of little people
clinging
to what
*little faith*                                        *Matthew 17:20
they knew...
of little faith
or victory o're sin,
as nagging shrews.

In You, oh LORD...
am I not more than this?
For if I'm not
then send me into
the deep abyss.                                       *Revelation 9:11

But now
an angel's touch
comes to me in the night,
pointing me to Living Water                           *John 7:37-39
and toward the Bread of Life.                         *John 6:48-50

I come and drink,                                     *Isaiah 55:1-2
am satisfied,
and hungering no more—                                *Matthew 5:6
am strengthened for a journey
forty days and nights in store...

before I seek                                    *Matthew 7:7-8
sweet refuge                                     *2 Samuel 22:3
in a whisper,
like a Balm                                      *Jeremiah 8:22
after wind,
and quake,
and fire
comes tearing pass me,
then a calm

will come over all my senses
calling me
to live for Christ,
letting His sweet sword of truth
cut through my soul just like a knife...         *Hebrews 4:12

deep down into the marrow
of my spirit, mind, and heart—
dividing all that's in me
until I am set apart...

For this, His will, I'll walk into
the winds, earthquakes, and fire
to shake the souls asleep                         *Ephesians 5:14
with a waking message DIRE...

that our God is
an all consuming flame                            *Hebrews 12:29
who burns the dross                                *Malachi 3:1-3
in lives so lost
who call upon His name.                            *Romans 10:13

# THE CORNERSTONE

Women were brought to Christ our LORD,
but His grace had struck a cord…

…among many people of His time
for He challenged all reason & rhyme.

One fell at His feet, shaken & torn--
as the object of unbridled scorn.

The mob held their stones,
eager to take aim--
certain the Master
would add to her shame.

But that He did not, oddly enough.
Instead he called their arrogant bluff.

"Those without sin can throw the first stone."
Then the mob left in a humbled tone.                    *John 8:1-11

But today stones still fly
this way and that…
with the same vicious venom
between dogs and cats.

Some say stones
can still be thrown
if the sin is BAD ENOUGH,
if a person's gay
or led astray
surely God has had enough!

"Oh my, oh me--
why shouldn't we
avenge our dear, sweet LORD?

Let's grab our gear
slice off an ear,
with our trusty sword!"                  *Matthew 26:51-54, Mark 14:47

Why wouldn't He appreciate
this message of intolerant hate...

that burns more bridges than it builds
and fuels our ego furnace til

that fateful day
come what may
when there'll BE NO place to hide--
not in the ocean,
through magic potions,
on land or over skies.

That day some will stand,
feeling less grand,
and taken down a notch...
when the sky turns black
like a cloth sack
and the moon's just a bloody blotch.          *Revelation 6:12-14

With the meek heir to earth,              *Psalm 37:11, Matthew 5:5
through a Great Rebirth,                  *John 3:1-13, 1 Peter 1:23
Holy Fire will reign from the Throne,              *Hebrews 12:29
and all will be avenged
by His baptismal singe...                          *Matthew 3:11
when Yahweh throws
          His Cornerstone.                         *Matthew 21:42

Author's Note:
I want to make one point undeniably clear, and that is that this piece
is NOT directed toward pastors who preach a doctrine of repentance
from sin: any and all sin, that is, up to and including the sin of same-
sex attraction in thought or deed. Rather, it is aimed at militant hate
groups who, through lies of omission, skirt divine truth; who give

the LGBTQ community the impression that they cannot be called to follow Christ. Truly, this is a heinous lie from hell. One might ask what makes true Christians any different from such groups, since we preach that gay people must turn from homosexuality? I will tell you the difference, unabashedly. The central message of hate groups to this sect of society is that God hates them, and there is no HOPE. But the message of The Gospel is that "...for God so loved the world, that He gave His only Son, that WHOSOEVER believes in Him may not perish but will have eternal life." (John 3:16) The LGBTQ Community is comprised of people who are just that, whosoevers. And through Christ, hope is *infinite!*

# THE INVITATION

You came without an invitation,
borrowed manger,                                    *Luke 2:7
borrowed tomb.                                      *Luke 23: 50-56
Come now, at this, our invocation.
This time we have made room.

Come here for there
are two or more
who've gathered in Your name;                       *Matthew 18:20
as You have promised
in Your Word,
on which we stake this claim:

that You are mighty, LORD, to save;                 *Zephaniah 3:17
that You have made a place...                       *John 14:3
where we, Your guests,          *Matthew 22:1-14, Luke 14:15-24
may be so blessed—
immersed in Your sweet grace!                       *Romans 13:14

Cause, LORD, it's been a journey long.
We are so weary now.
As eyes fall closed,
we're still & know,                                 *Psalm 46:10
You're God to Whom we bow.

So, we'll walk this valley
of death's shadow,
but we'll fear no evil there.                       *Psalm, Chapter 23
Because You've promised to be with us,
and to You we'll cast our cares.                    *1 Peter 5:7

This fallen world's
no home to us.
It's taken many tolls.
Now wipe our tears                                  *Revelation 21:4
as we draw near                                     *James 4:8
to Christ Who's saved our souls!                    *Romans 10:9

# THE LAUNDROMAT

*Mark 9:3

Last night
I dreamed that
I had run out
of clean clothes.

Then upon
stumbling                                    *Psalm 37:24
throughout the
darkened corners
of my closet
and under the
shadowy secrets
of my bed,
I finally found
my garments
scattered
all apart
in the dirt.

Having not a washer,
nor the time
for such a homey task
as hand-washing,
I was forced
to air my dirty laundry
before the public view.

So there I was.
I edged to the
local laundromat
and soon hurled
my ugly load
at the feet
of an old
washing machine.

Then I realized
that I'd forgot my wallet
and had nothing
in my
possession
to pay for the mess
that was
long since ground
into my clothing.

And I was all alone
in the empty room,
or so I thought.

That's when
a bent figure
appeared
from the corner
of my eyes.

His presence
startled me.
Ashamed,
I turned
to see Him.

*What is He doing here?*
I asked myself.
*Just standing there…*
*what does He wait for?*

That's when
my eyes caught His Own,
He had so bold eyes
that burned into my soul
and my heart sank.

Then He smiled
with lips parting
to say hello.

But questions hit me.
*What was wrong?*
*Why had I waited*
*so long to wash my clothing?*
Did He ask this
with His voice…
or through those
burning eyes                                    *Revelation 19:12
of His?

Had He asked at all?
Or had I asked myself?
I can't remember now.

But feeling pinned
to answer,
I offered an excuse
that just happened
to be true,

"I have no money
to pay for this load.
I left all
my belongings
behind today."

"Come,"
He said warmly,
"You can put them
in with Mine.
I also
left all My belongings
behind
and have little to spend,

but I will make
room for your own.
I don't mind
to pay for your load."

Flustered and confused,
but grateful—
I tossed my
filthy rags                                          Isaiah 64:6
into His washer.

Then I turned to this
new Friend                                           *John 15:15
with a remnant of
angst and guilt,
crying...

"HOW can I
EVER repay You?
You seem to have
so little, and yet
You still give.
And Your robe
is so clean and fresh...
as pure as the
Bright Morning Star!                            *Revelation 22:16
But mine—so dirty!
Won't they stain Your robe?
I've just never been
able
to get rid of
those stains
by myself."

His Word--                                           *John 1:1-4
it was
warm and loving,
as I began to wake,                              *Revelation 3:2

"Oh, Child,
can't you yet see?                                        *Matthew 13:16
Your DEBT
has already
BEEN PAID,                                               *Colossians 2:13-14
and
*everything*
comes clean
in My wash."                        *Psalm 51:7, Malachi 3:2, 1 John 1:7

Author's Note:
I wrote The Laundromat when I was around 14 years old, shortly
after Christ saved me. It was during my parent's divorce, when my
father had become a poor man. He and I would load up the pick up
trucks every Sunday, and head to the local laundromat to wash our
clothes together. The process reminded me of Christ's redemptive
work. What is important to note here, however, is that the salvation –
the cleansing, it wasn't "free." A price had to be paid. But it was HE
who paid it, in full, to redeem us. But that doesn't mean salvation
now costs us nothing. As you see in this poem, there was a struggle...a
sorrow over our condition, and a need for CHANGE. A change that
comes only through repentance, a very willful turning from the sin
and filth we once called home. And it wasn't "easy" to load that mess
into a truck and drive it somewhere. It wasn't always "entertaining"
to have to wait, as we in our struggles and perils have to wait upon
the LORD's deliverance at times. It wasn't fun to air my most private
matters before a myriad of unknown eyes. But it was NECESSARY.
And for it, I was cleansed to walk in the newness of life...eternally.

# THE MAN DELUSION

the **man** delusion
does not compute
it spins its wheels
in vile dispute

demanding evidence
pining for proof
it looks to beakers
instead of Truth                                    *John 14:6

ignoring One risen                                  *Mark 16:6
from the dead
ignoring, too,
the words in red

those, we'll avoid
at at each and every turn
for they ignite
Holy Fire, in return                                *Hebrews 12:29

we'll just pretend
that He never existed
and muddle through
with salvation resisted

and in the mean while
we'll try to buy
our worth in
plastic paradigms

the **man** delusion
is one that confounds
it runs it course
round and round:

poor in spirit, without hope
lacking proper Way to cope

mourning from its every loss
bitter, counting all the costs

meek enough to inherit earth
but never telling of its worth

a hunger that will not relent
rejecting all sweet nourishment

merciful to all its own,
but hateful to those unknown

pure enough in heart to try
but loosing sight of One so high

for making peace—we seldom care
except with sin, hate, and despair

longing to see some restitution
but fearing any persecution

instead, adore weak platitudes
that don't reflect beatitudes

keep seeking love that can't be found
in money spent or fame renowned

yet this **man** delusion
says there's no rod
to fall
from saying,
"There's no God."                                          *Psalm 14:1

Author's note:

The writer of Hebrews 11:1 define faith in this manner: "Now faith is the substance of things hoped for, the evidence of things not seen." So the issue is this: say you had some rock-solid, undeniable, irrefutable scientific evidence of God's existence...well, you might have a fine thing there. But if it is on this physical evidence that you base your belief in Christ, then *by definition*, whatever you have would no longer be based on FAITH. And what does the Scripture tell us? "...without faith, it is impossible to please God." (Hebrews 11:6)

# THE PLANT

Once a woman received
a large, flowery plant as a gift.
It beautiful, and she
she was very proud of it.                              *Proverbs 16:18

But after time,
because of circumstances
that were beyond her control,
the plant got stuck
in a dark corner                                       *John 3:19
of the patio.
Light could not reach it, then
**old man winter**
slithered in
and sat around,
its icy breath
in a silent coil
around the branches.

By the time she noticed
the plant again
in the springtime,
it was barely recognizable.
Its branches were cracked and gray.
It had no flowers, or even leaves—
much less, *fruit*.                                    *Galatians 5:22-23
And its warped, scaly limbs
stuck out like
crooked thorns.                          *Matthew 13:7, Mark 4:7, Mark 8:7

But when she looked closer,
at the base of the plants—near the roots,
she saw that it was green! She thought,
"How can this be? How can
there be life

in something
so seemingly dead?"
Still, the plant was ugly.
It did not fit in
with her plans
for a new garden,
and she even considered
throwing it away.

Now, even though this plant
had been given to her
as a gift
and was not for her
to waste,
it was mainly for the sake of
the her own hopes
and her own dreams
of a new garden
that it was spared
for a time
from the fire.                                                      *John 15:6

So she put it in the Light...                                  *John 8:12
and let the rain fall on it.                         *Deuteronomy 32:2
She didn't know what to expect,
or even what to hope for.
Whether or not
the plant would grow again
was beyond her control.
She could not
*pry into*
those branches, with her
mere mortal hands,
and pull the sap
from the roots to the tips—
no matter
*how much*
she wanted
it to be *saved*.                                                *Titus 3:5

She just knew that plants
cannot refuse the Light.                                            *John 8:12
They crave it.
They grow toward It
*instinctively*
for warmth and nourishment.

Can I tell you what
happened to her surprise?
After taking in the Light,                                          *John 8:12
with the rain,                                               *Deuteronomy 32:2
little green buds began to pop
out of gray, cracked branches!
It was a tiny miracle to see.
Now pure green-gold
is fusing through
those old, dry stalks.

And she *has faith*                                              *Hebrews 11:6
the plant
will bloom again.

Author's Note:
*The Light is our God, Jesus.*
*The rain is your teaching.*
*The plant is His church.*
*The branches are the congregations.*
*Keep lighting your Light shine, Pastors,*
*and branches...*
*will bend.*

# THE QUICKENING

A tiny little flutter
stirs from deep inside
-*she questions*-
as it startles her,
and she does not know why...

at first,
where it has come from
just prompting there within-
jumps, abounds, and stops
so soon before it starts again.

This tiny bit of Life,                                        *John 14:6
it jolts
within the bride;                                    *Ephesians 5:22-33
she cannot sleep
with hunger deep                                          *Matthew 5:6
for Bread                                                    *John 6:35
    & *meat*            *Hebrews 5:12, 1 Corinthians 3:2
    & wine.                            *Matthew 26:27-29

So it's not her own
-this *movement* now-
it comes while she
lay *still*;                                            *Psalm 46:10
comes as she pines and waits;                           *Isaiah 40:31
and watches;                                *Matthew 24:42, Mark 13:35
for it to beat at will.

And then she knows,
it's all so clear
-laughing-                                             *Genesis 18:12
she'll realize...
that God has breathed                                   *Genesis 2:7
into her womb
and has called one to rise.

As cells divide
like ancient seas;                                    *Exodus 14:21
as Lazarus
was raised;                                           *John 11:43-44
as storms were silenced
on the spot
and all stood so amazed.           *Matthew 8:23-27, Mark 4:35-41

Who has this voice,
authority-
calling life at His command?
Who stirs us from
a deadly rest
to ask
*how*
we can withstand…

this gentle nudge,
this fleeting twinge,
this stirring
from down deep…
this quest
to want Him more and more
that wakes us
          from our sleep.                            *Ephesians 5:14

It grows and grows
as time goes on,
as hunger
          drives her – craving…
like mad
for whatever she can find
to satiate the raving.

And much is offered up for her
in this her time of need
by well-intentioned
passers-by,

so on what will she feed?

Spend wages
for what does not satisfy                               *Isaiah 55:2
as she whines and thirsts...?
Will she incline
itching ears                                           *2 Timothy 4:3
to die,
and take advice
that's worse...

to pay for what
was never Bread...                                     *John 6:48-50
to starve with
good news
left unread.

What does she want...?
Or does she covet...                                   *Deuteronomy 7:25
a little god,
so she can love it?

One who won't demand too much,
but will lend a healing touch.

One who stays out of her way,
and hasn't really much to say.

One that leaves her dead in sin
that she loves more, along with men.                    *John 12:43

One who never challenges
her thoughts, and dreams – beliefs...
one who plays it safe,
and that she can neatly leave...

right in her back pocket,
pulling out to show and tell -
one who never stops her cold
or sends someone to hell.

A nice and tidy god
she wants,
one fit for all occasion-
one who won't offend too much
or won't compromise persuasion.

And yet a Father
waits in the wings
of this situation, dire—
for He knows exactly what
His Baby                                                      *John 3:1-3
will require...

EVERYTHING
-the bottom line-
right down to her marrow,
for her surrender
of own life
just as a falling sparrow.                              *Matthew 10:29

So she'll toss, but turn...
while she does learn
          to be a proper host
of Life within
and then attend
to just what matters most:

hard labor                                  *1 Thessalonians 1:2-5
and her sacrifice,                                        *1 Peter 2:5
with these she'll make the mark...
not by desire
of what the flesh aspires                          *Ephesians 2:3
in a world
lukewarm, and dark.                              *Revelation 3:16

Until then this little movement
everyday it grows,
just like the pining question
Nicodemus came to pose...                              *John 3:4

But who can hear it?                            *Matthew 13:16-17
'Cept those born of the Spirit                            *John 3:6
        for it comes just like the wind...               *John 3:8
and we have no power
of the place or the hour                          *Matthew 24:36
        when Christ will
                *come again.*                     *Revelation 22:20

# THE SHROUD MAN

We rest
in a pasture
with clouds overhead.
They glide
in soft splendor
o'er the living and dead.

We watch
in quiet muse
the shapes they create,
shifting above us
in a gradual gait.

We try
        to surmise
the whims of the skies,
as edges of clouds
            drift and scrimmage.
And if we rely
        on our mere mortal eyes,
            we spot only an ash
            graven image.                    *Exodus 20:4

For our own perception
has suffered deception,
        and left us unable to see            *Matthew 13:14-15
what has true form
apart from the norm
        of all that we know and believe.

But should God let us spy
through lit beams of His eyes
        a vision of gold is revealed—

from an old linen cloth
uneaten by moth
    comes a *Truth*                                 *John 14:6
        no tomb could conceal!
And His silver lining
dawns a star                                   *Revelation 22:16
    so refining...                         *Malachi 3:3, 1 Peter 1:7

...that its great gleam must
be sent to redeem us.

So we'll wait
in slow wonder
at the billowing thunder
    created by some sonic boom—
'neath a moon
red as wine
dark as blood, so divine,                           *Acts 2:20
fearing not
    any damning or doom.

*Escaped from Turin!*
And coming again—
    to tear apart
    our imagined cloud man,
straight down from Heaven
comes *Sweet Manna*—unleavened          *John 6:33
    unfolding as...
    the "Shroud Man."

Author's Note:
Years ago, I was intrigued by an article about the infamous Shroud
of Turin, a piece of cloth that many believe to be the actual burial
shroud of the Messiah—Jesus Christ. As a Christian, at first I was
a little offended, because the author kept referring to the image
merely as "Shroud Man." It struck me as being irreverent...after all,
He came to a lost world and redeemed the sins of all humanity to a
Holy God, only to be called a "Shroud Man?" But it occurred to me

that just as the Shroud of Turin itself is a mystery, the earthly life of our LORD was (and is) still a mystery to many. So the imagery for this poem came to me. I pictured children (like God's children everywhere) laying on a field discerning shapes in the distant clouds. And I recalled that Christ said He would come in the clouds (Mark 13:26, Revelation 1:7). So the ash graven image, our "imagined cloud man" in this poem represents our idolatry and worship of false prophets. But our returning Christ is presented as the Sweet Manna from Heaven, literally – the Bread of Life that was without "leaven," or sin. But the authenticity of such a piece of cloth is largely irrelevant to my faith. That's because my faith is centered on the finished work of Christ on Calvary, His resurrection, and the tangible change this has brought about in my own life. But I think of the Shroud of Turin is a beautiful mystery, to be sure!

# THE STORM

It's been a dark and stormy night,
and I – no lantern by.
I muddle through the cold, dark damp
and curse the winds so high.

They swirl right round me,
howling near;
engulf my limbs
and hasten fear.

And in them I have lost
all that once was mine,
as I fumble through the fury
of my Maker's wrath, divine.

How could He lead me here
into this cruel abyss?
Why does He hide His face                    *Psalm 88:14
from sight and leave me in all this?

But it's not for me to know,
the wheres and hows and whys.        *1 Corinthians 13:12
It's only for me to trust
He'll calm the writhing skies.     *Matthew 8:23-27, Mark 4:35-41

In this we must have faith
and withstand the tempest's tide,
to follow the sovereign God
on Whom we have relied.

For even in the raging uproar
of this world's violent loss,
we'll persevere                              *Galatians 6:9
and draw near                                   *James 4:8
to know the one who bore the cross...      *Galatians 3:13

because it's known that
in our suffering
of lost and lonely days,
that coil around to snare us
in a gray-dimmed, chain-link maze...

there's still a light that shines                    *John 8:12
through blackening, brutal gales.
There is a guiding hand,
and a love that never fails.                    *1 Corinthians 13:13

# THE TROUBLE WITH BAND-AIDS

*Jeremiah 6:14

A wound has occurred
and because we care,
we slap on a band-aid
and do not dare…

ever remove it
or stop to check
if it is working
or if it's a wreck.

We take for granted
that band-aids don't heal.
They only cover
our nasty ordeals.

And often times
they serve
only to slow,
the healing process,
as infection grows.

And since we can't see
the scar as it festers,
we compound the problem
with more loving gestures.

Like new colorful band-aids
of unique design—
thinking they'll distract
us from pain, now confined.

And week after week
all our sorrows

remain—
through ski trips and socials
and choral refrain.

We try to ignore it,
we want to pretend…
that band-aids restore it
so we can defend…

the lack of time spent
and attention paid
to the source of injury
and the mess we have made…

from smothering a cut
that runs far too deep…
saved only
        by blood
                *coming soon*                    *Revelation 22:7-12
                as it seeps…

in gradual expense
through the bandage, it keeps
spilling out to cleanse
the disease that we reap.                         *Galatians 6:7

Til we are
Abel                                                    *Genesis 4:4
to see                                             *Matthew 13:16
        a new course
of *action* to heal
this wound at its source,

and rip off the band-aids
from top to bottom,
with a burning of flesh
that will rival old Sodom!                    *Genesis, Chapter 19

But first, call the Doctor...                    *Matthew 9:12
the One in the Book
and lend wounds over
to *Him*
for a look.

He will tell you the Truth,                       *John 14:6
that wounds should be exposed...
to the Bright Morning Light                   *Revelation 22:16
and fresh scent of a Rose.              *Song of Solomon 2:1

# A VERY IMPORTANT DATE

Running so late for her wedding
in the streets and surely heading...

down any old cold dark alley
and back-sliding in the valley,

seeking detours that can't be found
taking direction so unsound.

Unprepared
     for the Judgment Day
the bride                                                          *Ephesians 5:22-32
     has lost sight of her Way.                          *John 14:6

So she waits and pines instead
by the graves, among the dead...

longing for some sweet release
she finds no joy,
     strength,
       or peace.

She hungers for her wedding feast,
but lies
     as bait for the stray beast...

who roams all about to devour                                     *1 Peter 5:8
the bride and maids until the hour—

will come
     to take them
       off the streets
from all corners
and scorching heat.

But just as a coin is tossed,                          *Luke 15:-10
then rolls away lost...

or one sheep leave the fold                            *Luke 15:4-7
with its fate so untold...

the Rightful Owner
        will comb the world
to claim
        His chosen
                treasure and pearl.                   *Matthew 13:44-46

So how much more precious
is a bride,                                            *Ephesians 5:25-27
despite what all
she tries to hide?

The Groom will cover every ground
till what belongs to Him is found.

He has the time and grace to wait
right up until the coming date...

and when that hour is round at last,
there will be no longer need to fast.   *Matthew 9:15, Mark 2:19
No darkened sky or shadows cast
will drown the call of trumpets' blast.           *Matthew 24:31
And once He's ventured out into
those last few streets for love that's true...     *Matthew 22:9

then wedding bells will sound                       *Revelation 19:7
so loud—
the dead will rise from ground.            *1 Thessalonians 4:16

All to witness these wedding vows
and mysteries we'll know somehow...

so she will find that Sacred Gate!                    *John 10:7-9
Though she was lost, He's never late.               *Galatians 4:4

# THE WOUNDING ROSE

(A poem for our daughter,
Doni, who has Autism.)


I happened cross a fragrant rose;
it's glory caught my eye.
And so I stopped to gaze with joy
in pleasant new surprise.

I held her beauty in my arms
and leaned in close enough
to let her grace envelope me
until I feel in love...

with such a tender presence
in her peace & stately charm
that I took hold
& branches scold
me with a sudden harm.

The thorns I did not see
had drawn my blood so quick
before I knew
just what to do
with this flower I'd chose to pick.

I was so shocked
and caught off guard,
at times wanting to concede.
But for her sweet love, haunting me—
she, I could never leave!

Kneeling by the wounding rose
I nursed a bloodstained palm,
but soon recovered
and discovered
my purpose in the calm.

Now I care for many roses,
in gardens that God adorns...
because I learned
that roses yearn
to be loved despite their thorns.

# THERE I GO AGAIN

There I go again;
quick to stumble,                                    *Matthew 18:8
break, and fall.                                     *Proverbs 16:18
Another choice of word
that's slipped and heard
so full of swearing gall.

And there I go again:
poor steward of time and wages;            *1 Corinthians 4:2
so wasted, spent;
dare I repent
before the Rock of Ages?                         *Psalm 18:2

Now there I go again:
harboring rage against my neighbor,
whom I'm to love                                  *Matthew 22:39
if I'm made of
the Spirit for Whom I labor.

God of Heaven,
tell me this—
do I betray You
with a kiss...                    *Matthew 26:48-49, Mark 14:44-45

from unclean lips                                  *Isaiah 6:5
so coarse—profane?
I am not fit to
call Your name!

Much less to have Your mercy, new,        *Lamentations 3:22-23
that falls on me with mourning due...        *2 Corinthians 7:10

so crisp and clean,
'fore men confessed                               *James 5:16
are all my sins
as grace refreshed;

and Godly sorrow swallows pride
with
I AM                                                          *Exodus 3:14, Mark 14:62
holy—satisfied,

not by a pious claim of mine
for none are there to find.                                   *Romans 3:23
Though of no merit,
I will inherit
a Kingdom, most divine!

Because God's rage against me
has been meted out;
and not on me
but on a tree                                                 *Galatians 3:13
where Christ defeated doubt!

And so to Him I reach,
despite my deep chagrin…
His hem, I touch,                                             *Mark 5:25-34
absolving much!
It's *there,* I go again.

# TO THIRST

As darkness encroaches,
consuming the sun...
with hate conquering love,
seems the enemy's won.

And tempers, they rise
like a tsunami's tide.

Then greed drives me to covet,
such that I'm not above it.

And with each new temptation,
my flesh is so pleased...
but these are mere symptoms
of a greater disease.

I thirst                                          *Matthew 5:6
while alone
in the barren, dry fields.
I chase
aft' God's throne
and long to be healed.

Dare I come to His fountain                       *Isaiah 55:1
in my weakened distress...?
when I've so many burdens
and sins to confess...?

I have spent all my wages
like the Prodigal Son.                            *Luke 15:11-32
I have wasted sweet grace                         *Romans 6:1-2
and deserve to be shun.

Still Christ calls me to Him
like a star who welcomes night,
as He dresses my wounds
as grief is crushed under His might.

I drink
from His fountain,
so perfect, unflawed...                                    *John 7:37-39
I burst
into song                                                       *Psalm 118:14
with joy that trees applaud.                           *Isaiah 55:12

For I craved
through the fight                                             *1 Timothy 6:12
when brooding pangs overpowered...
but was saved
by His light                                                     *John 8:12
in this, my eleventh hour.                         *Matthew 20:1-16

# TO THOSE WHO LOVE GOD

No white picket fence,
where all was fine…
I came from chaos
and fear, sublime.

I heard the screaming
vicious names;
I felt the rage –
adulterous games.

I knew no peace
or so I thought,
'cept through prayer
more things were wrought…

than I had dreamed of
from a little bed,
asking my God
Who once had said:

all things are possible                    *Matthew 19:26
with Him alone.
A child, I went boldly
to His throne.                              *Hebrews 4:16

And He calmed the
storm in me,
pursued me when
I tried to flee.

Convicted me when
I would need it,
called me to know
His Word and heed it.

I grew to be a woman, still,
that knows His voice and seeks His will.

I called to Him, my Adonai,
begging for love from the Most High.                    *Psalm 91:1

And I was given
a strong, true man—
who loved me back,
who took my hand...

and placed on it a golden band—
as time would tell, he would withstand...

the sling and arrows
of my whim
and love me still
when hope was slim.

This man restored me
to the full...
like God, the soul,
like kings to rule                                      *Ephesians 5:22-23

not with an iron thumb or fist
with but a soft and tender kiss,                        *Ephesians 5:25-27

he led me out of desert halls,
he broke the chains of prison walls...

put life inside
and let it grow,
with pride and joy
that over flows...

so no more pain am I to nurse.
My God is breaking every curse.                         *Exodus 20:5-6

# TREES

Tree of knowledge
tree of life...
forbidden fruit                                    *Genesis 2:9
that caused such strife.

Tempting woman,
testing man
& yet we ask
was this God's plan?

How could He let
such tragedies -
as famines, floods,
atrocities...

bear down on us infernally,
leaving some to die eternally?

To roast within the second death        *Revelation 20:14
the lake of fire that's satan's breath...  *Revelation 20:10

how can it be, this God is *just?*
But question Him, oh, if we must –

and find just what the prophets say
about the Potter and His clay:                    *Isaiah 64:8

How there came a Man of sorrows,              *Isaiah 53:3
same yesterday and tomorrow...            *Hebrews 13:8

Who walked among us in our grief               *John 1:14
and felt it, too, with no relief...        *Hebrews 4:15

from torturous wounds by which we're healed -    *Isaiah 53:5
this gospel truth has been revealed...

to hearts as humble as a child,                          *Matthew 18:4
first to the Jew and then gentile:

He came despite the pain afflicted;
He came as all servants predicted;
He came beside the thief and whore;                 *Luke 23:39-42
He came while temple veil was tore...               *Matthew 27:51

He comes again to old dry bones,                    *Ezekiel 37:1-10
breathing new life straight from the Throne;
He comes to us for this and more,
bringing a balm – our soul's restore;                 *Jeremiah 8:22
He comes though we welcome Him not,
purveying peace where we have fought;
He comes to burn away the dross,                       *Malachi 3:3
if we but take up our own cross...      *Matthew 16:24-26, Luke 9:23

And He will come to wipe our tears,                  *Revelation 21:4
renew our faith – assuage our fears;
And He will come to celebrate,
a wedding feast – an open Gate;          *Revelation 19:9, John 10:9
And He will come to reconcile
worlds that once, Him had reviled;                  *Romans 11:25-32
And He will come as trumpets call,                *1 Corinthians 15:52
the quick and dead, as Judge of all!                   *2 Timothy 4:1

So when we suffer in despair
and Him might question, "Is he – where?"
Know this much with darkness nigh,
Who suffered *most* is the...Most High.                    *Psalm 91:1

For on a third, dark blood-stained tree                *Galatians 3:13
He sealed our fates eternally...

Giving of grace that's so profound –
a pardon, pass, to holy ground...

one we can't steal, earn, buy, or sell!          *Ephesians 2:8-9
What Eve had lost when Adam fell!          *Genesis, Chapter 3

As filthy rags, our best works lie,          *Isaiah 64:6
our hearts are sick, our bodies die…    *Jeremiah 17:9, Genesis 3:19

but still, He comes amid the rift
'tween God and man with hallowed Gift –          *John 3:16

for in His place, there was no ram          *Genesis 22:13
to sacrifice, only the Lamb.          *1 Peter 1:19

How much is Love? What is the cost…?
to ransom we who are so lost…?          *Mark 10:45

And Who would give Himself and Child
to butchery and loathsome guile…?

'Cept One Who Saves and intercedes,
Who has felt all our wanton needs –          *Hebrews 4:14-15

so qualified, this Advocate,          *1 John 2:1
our case, He pleads, from where He sits

by Adonai, at His right hand…          *Mark 16:19
as Son of God and Son of Man.

# TURNING POINT

confined to die,
so tired and worn
with all my losses
that I mourn                                           *Matthew 5:4

a life so spent
and wasted time
I look back now
no reason, rhyme

the myriad of my mistakes,
the chances lost – the toll they take

where am I headed…?
which path to travel…?
as night creeps in,
as dreams unravel

into a lazy yesteryear,
fusing within a fallen tear

that trickles down my lonely cheek
where beauty's gone, where future's bleak

a memory is youth and hope
I cry inside, pretend to cope

what is a man or woman kind?
what purpose can we strive to find?

if all we are is ash and dust…                        *Genesis 3:19
then who, are we, in whom to trust?

if this is all and nothing more,
who stands beside an open Door…?                      *John 10:9

and does not enter, does not seek
a strength that's offered to the weak?                    *2nd Corinthians 12:9

For all will fail, all will be lost
like ships under a tempest tossed

if we don't look across the waves
and reach out for the One Who Saves                           *Acts 4:12

for in the darkness shines a Light                            *John 8:12
an outstretched hand, a strength and might,

that raises us from certain death
that sparks to life sweet baby's breath                       *John 3:1-3

of a new soul who yearns for God,                     *2 Corinthians 5:17
a Sower's seed,                                          *Matthew 13:8
a Shepherd's rod                                          *Psalm 23:4

a narrow Way,                                            *Matthew 7:14
a still small voice                                     *1 Kings 19:12
that whispers we must make a choice

between this fate - so caustic, grim…
and one of joy with hope in Him                               *John 15:11

# TWILIGHT TIME

darkness falls
descends on me

       from time to time
       with no relief

immediate, in my sight
as my soul cries out for the Light                  *John 8:12

       I am alone in present grief
       I am apart from my beliefs

the enemy has sought me out
& stolen from me, joy - as doubt                *John 10:10

       like some cold fog surrounding me
       my once sweet soul, abounding free

now broken by pain, so unrelenting
no God, no more...no use repenting

       or so it tempts me, leads me astray
       to think the sun has lost its rays

to think the ocean has no waves
to think a prophet has no cave               *1 Kings 19:9

       to hide oneself, take shelter there
       for a small voice, still whisper where      *1 Kings 19:12

we are questioned to our core
of whereabouts and so much more...

       where are we in our angst and pain?
       where are we in our sin, abstained?

where are we in the desert heat?
where are we in our soul's defeat?

"Where are *you*, Child?" This Present Friend...          *John 15:15
seeks to know us more just when

    we are so lost and so alone,
    but calls us boldly 'fore His Throne!          *Hebrews 4:16

For He was tempted, tried but true          *Hebrews 4:15
& lives again to make us new          *2 Corinthians 5:17

come wind and earthquake,
fire and flood -
all mere precursors
to His blood...

    that's spilled for each and every one
    who turn from self and toward the Son

yes, in my sorrows, fear – unrest
there comes a Shepherd's call, request

    to follow Him and hear His voice...          *John 10:27
    beseeching me to make a choice

I welcome Him, my soul cries out
and I'm delivered from all doubt

    how do we see?
    how can we hear?

With His warm touch,
that's always near...          *James 4:8
that opens eyes and
hearts and ears...          *Matthew 13:16

that cradles us in sweet relief,
restores our souls amid the grief

  of earthly life so frail and fleeting
  of failures past & sin competing

for our attention, time, and souls...
until the fateful church bell tolls...

  right up until that present hour
  when we submit to Higher Power

and see the Light            *John 8:12
to which we bend,
from desert heat...
this gentle Wind             *John 3:8

  will whisper still to us again
  our LORD & Master, God & Friend!    *John 15:15

# UNFOLDING FAITH

Down in a pit
of ash and dust
I cry to You, Most High…                                    *Psalm 91:1
so oft' I've asked,
of cares I cast,                                            *1 Peter 5:7
You let me suffer – *why?*

For all things
come by Your will,
sunshine and rain…                                         *Matthew 5:45
grace to be still.                                          *Psalm 46:10

And so in my calamity
it's hard to see the Light                                  *John 8:12
of the world,
as dreams unfurl,
and like a sickness – night…

falls on me
in dreary fog
through which I cannot see                                  *Matthew 13:14-15
and hope seems dim,
I sink –- not swim,
in muddied waters misery.

Held captive
to my fears, to past mistakes, to shame…
and consequence
that makes no sense
but who have I to blame?

Except for self,
ambition, wealth;
for this I call Your throne?
My mortal cares

these are a snare
to faith that I must hone...

For what had Abraham,
'cept a promise as stars and sand?                    *Genesis 22:17
And where had His head to lay...
as One called the Son of Man?                              *Luke 9:58

What had Moses
but a desert bush of flame?                    *Exodus, Chapter 3
What right had he of
the Great I AM                              *Exodus 3:14, Mark 14:62
to even know His name?

What had Sarah but a laugh
in shock and in dismay,
that God would breathe life
to her womb –
'spite age that came her way?                    *Genesis 18:1-15

What had Noah...when
not a single drop of rain had struck
to prove his claim
or save his name,
but an ark he did construct!                    *Genesis, Chapters 5-7

What had Jacob but a ladder                    *Genesis 28:10-17
or Joseph but a dream?                          *Genesis, Chapter 37
What had the Psalmist but
green pastures and still streams?                    *Psalm 23:2

What had Rahab
but holy fear –                                        *Joshua 2:8-13
the fear of a God she'd heard...
had dried the seas,
brought kings to knees,
captured cities at His Word?

So what have I, my God, in this?
But a promise to my soul...                    *Philippians 1:6
and that You'll keep
whether I lay sleep
or wake to see it unfold.

# VALENTINE

In my sorrow and my grief,
the hardest thing can be belief.

For all my fears, they plague me now
like some demented, sacred cow.          *Exodus 32, Chapter 32

Have I no hope? For I feel lost,
by some seducing temptress tossed...

another god of wood and stone                    *Exodus 20:3
as philosophic psyches drone,

and
I am
LEFT...so all alone,
until I bow before the Throne!

For there is grace,
abounding love
that cradles me...
this selfless Dove!

He died for doubters
just as I,
He died for those who murder, lie...

and for a certain fancy few
who sit, all smiles, within the pew!

They never cry, never repent.
They never knell or have time spent...

wailing inside an inner room,                    *Matthew 6:6
DESPERATE – wanting just their Groom...          *John 3:29

but lie
in dungeons of keyless cages—
a prim, private pain, where ever rages…

a whitewashed soul                                    *Matthew 23:27-28
and freshly painted,
white picket fences, so unacquainted…

with Adonai, not yet, at least,
until comes round His final feast…

because His table will be filled                      *Luke 14:16-24
with honest hearts
who've prayed until

all pride has gone before the fall                    *Proverbs 16:18
of man, from God there comes a call:

Go touch His wounds,
He gives them here!                                   *John 20:24-29
Come feel the pain
sin caused Him, Dear…

it is for you that He now waits—
a faithful Shepherd,                                  *John 10:14-16
an open gate.

And all your hate
for Him, He knows.
You've many questions – answered slow.

But when it's hard to see through dark,
He is the swift, uplifting spark…

a holy flame that ever burns,                         *Hebrews 12:29
and for your love, that ever yearns!

For you, He died, loves you as wife...                    *Ephesians 5:25-33
but leave you now, with this, your life.

And it is your's, I will not take it...
but I call that you forsake it –                          *Matthew 16:25

and go with Him
where 'ere He leads,
His humble flock
for you to feed...

on just His Word                                          *John 6:35
and Spirit more,
Sweet Virgin Bride,
He does adore...

unlike some vile and painted harlot                       *Revelation17:3-6
whose robes, in blood, have become scarlet.

But with incessant pleas to repent,
Christ's blood was spilled – God's anger spent...         *Isaiah 53:10

and not in wrath on mankind more,
but on the cross – the veil He tore!                      *Matthew 27:51

He lifts your's now for all
to see                                                    *Matthew 13:16
your yearning gleam, His fallen knee.

So by His wounds that set you free,                       *1 Peter 2:24
be His, His love, His Bride to be.                 *Revelation 19:7-9; 21:9

# WE ALL WANT TO BE A MOSES

We all want to be a Moses
at one time or another,
until arms fall down in battle
and must be held up by our brothers.                    *Exodus 17:12-14

We all want to be a Shadrach,
taking pride                                                      *Proverbs 16:18
in our conviction;
that is until
at God's will
we're in the furnace of affliction.                      *Daniel 3:16-28

We all want to be a Mary
with expectant joy of our Good News
until we're on a lonely trek
that has no room for our views.                              *Luke 2:7

And what audience did Mary have
to applaud her piety?
Just ox and sheep,
a shepherd's keep,
of the simplest variety.

Who saw her there
in labor, bare?
On what platform did she speak?
A manger of hay,
and a donkey's bray,
for what else did she seek?

And what about Meshach?
What did Abednego have to prove?
Was their stance
by any chance
in hopes of a career move?

We long for signs                                  *Matthew 16:4, Luke 11:29
of grand design...
we pine for the still small whisper;                      *1 Kings 19:11-13
beside peaceful streams                                        *Psalm 23:2
and hope for dreams                                       *Genesis 37:1-11
without the nightmare of a cistern.                          *Genesis 37:19

We want to be so great
and we want to be so grand.
Like diamonds, shine!
Sought after, mined!
When we're just a grain of sand.

And therein lies the difference
between our hearts and Moses...
a difference we must learn
before another chapter closes.

Pride goes before a fall,                                    *Proverbs 16:18
a haughty spirit before disaster.
When seeking glory
from God's story
are we greater than our Master?             *Matthew 10:24, Luke 6:40

Are we prepared to taste of death?
With every honor-seeking breath?
For we know not what we covet...
Denied Promised Land,                                     *Numbers 20:1-13
will our faith wan
or hope to rise above it?

Who is Abel...                                               *Genesis 4:3-4
at God's table
from all the ages spanned
the cup, to drink,                  *Matthew 20:20-28, Matthew 26:39
or presume to think
they're to sit at God's right hand?                    *Hebrews, Chapter 1

For in the stillness of our hearts  *Jeremiah 17:9
resides the Rock of Ages...  *1 Corinthians 10:4
Who wrestles with man  *Genesis 32:22-32
til we understand
that death's a product of sin's wages.  *Romans 6:23

And so what of this faith business?
Do we still want to be called
if a life of humble servitude
fighting sin
just might be all?

Suppose we have no ministry
of the sort that brings us fame?
Suppose it's only
God and hell
Who ever knows our name?

For a life of words
that seemed unheard
made Jeremiah cry.  *Jeremiah 13:17
Paul was jailed;  *Acts 16:25
Barabbas – hailed;  *Matthew 27:17-26
Job struggled then he died.  *Job 19:26; 42:17

"Oh that my words were written
in a book," Job said in obscure grief.  *Job 19:23-24
With only his Redeemer  *Job 19:25
to witness his firm belief.

We all what to be a Moses.
But do we want despair?
Now Dreamers, wake—  *Ephesians 5:14
and step up to take
our cross Christ calls to bear.  *Matthew 16:24-26

# WHAT GOD SAYS TO ME

I asked of God,
"How long I'll wait?"
For dreams of mine
seem stalled by fate.
He would not tell
the time, it's length…
but said that I'll
renew my strength.                                    *Isaiah 40:31

I asked of God,
"What must I do?"
To earn His grace
that makes me new?                          *2ⁿᵈ Corinthians 5:17
He would not tell
me that I can,
but said it's finished                                 *John 19:30
by the Son of Man.                                    *Acts 7:56

I asked of God,
"What should I have?"
Like knowledge, tongues,
or faith and deeds?
He said that love
is foremost
what I will need.                              *1 Corinthians 13:1-3

I asked of God,
"What am I to be?"
According to His will?
He said to know
that He is God,
and simply to be still.                               *Psalm 46:10

I asked of God
"How am I do know Him?"

What ways has He preferred?
In visions, signs,
or thoughts of mine?
And He said just in His Word.                    *2nd Timothy 3:16-17


What Grace is Like

God's grace is like
    a gentle wind                                    *John 3:8
    that soothes our wayward souls,
it cradles us
despite the fuss
    of all that's taken tolls.

God's grace is like
    an unbruised reed,
    a dimly burning wick—                          *Isaiah 42:3
that's not snuffed out
despite our doubt
    and hearts that are so sick.                   *Jeremiah 17:9

God's grace is like a *treasure*, found!          *Matthew 13:44
A living water river...              *Isaiah 55:1, John 4:14; 7:37-38
    that flows to drench,
    our thirsts to quench                          *Matthew 5:6
      as a tender lover's quiver.

God's grace is like a *precious* pearl            *Matthew 13:45-46
of exquisite price—
    no matter the cost,
    to save the lost
while the cock crowed thrice...                   *Mark 14:72

for grace is love and truth, in one,
    a favor we cannot merit;                       *Ephesians 2:8-9
but only savor
without waver
    and answer a call...to share it.               *Acts 1:8

# WHAT HAPPENS WHEN...

What happens when
the doldrums come
and points of faith
just make me numb...?

When happens when
the mourning due
hangs like a fog—
when I'm untrue...

to all I think and know and feel;
to all that I've believed is real...?

What then
when
I am
fallen, lost;
when'
nothing's worth
the time or cost...?

What will I do?
Where will I turn?
From sin
or then
to all I've yearned?

For dreams of mine
like fading time
have vanished with no trace...
of their seeds;
just aching needs
in the hollow of their place.

What must I learn--?
What trial to pass--?
Can help me face
the looking glass...?                      *1 Corinthians 13:12

that's clouded, grim,
while failure looms
with aspirations
ne'er to bloom...?

Where is Hope?
How am I to cope?
When Heaven drowns with rain...?            *Matthew 5:45
Or could it be
my dream's set free
and may not die in vain...?

While hidden in the cleft of rock           *Exodus 33:19-23
where they can scarcely see
a coming Son
so pure
to lure
their branches                              *John 15:15
grown through He--

who calms the storms        *Matthew 8:22-27, Mark 4:35-41
and walks the sea;                          *Matthew 14:25-28
whose grace can save                         *Ephesians 2:8-9
a wretch like me;

who brought salvation
through the Jews;                            *John 4:22
whose resurrection                          *John 11:25-26
is Good News.

What happens when
I trust in Him?
What darkened sky
casts shadows, dim,

enough to hide a precious pearl          *Matthew 13:45
or dull His bright light of the world?          *John 8:12

What happens when
the death of dreams
and all I've longed for
just really seems

to make me die
to sin and self
is when treasure's found          *Matthew 13:44
in Heaven's wealth.

What happens is
that life I mourned          *Matthew 5:4
can't hold a candle
to this one, reborn!          *John 3:1-13

# WHAT I AM SAID TO BE

I grew up thinking I had to be
all that the world required of me.

To be "good,"
moral and just—
for goodness sake,
as such I must...

be sugar and spice
and everything "nice,"
with health
and wealth
despite its vice...

I should be busy,
and chase the wind—                                    *Ecclesiastes 2:26
whether vain,
or just remain
a failure in the end.

I've hoped for immortality,
and fancied what I am to be.
I've pined for fame
in my own name...
while idol plans don't part my sea.                    *Exodus 14:21-22

And so,
I turn,
and look to Christ.
I see                                                  *Matthew 13:16
a tree:                                                *Galatians 3:13
my sin – its price.                              *1 Corinthians 6:20

As a smoldering wick – a tender reed;                  *Isaiah 42:1-4
I ponder, now, what I'm to be:

poor in heart, that I might see                          *Matthew 5:8
God in His glory, eternally;

still and knowing He is God,                             *Psalm 46:10
not rushing after void facades;

broken-hearted that He might near,                       *Psalm 34:18
gaining wisdom with righteous fear;                      *Proverbs 9:10

weak that, in Him, I might be strong;        *2nd Corinthians 12:9-10
meek that, the earth, to me belongs;                     *Matthew 5:5

a branch that clings to the holy vine,                   *John 15:1-11
bearing good fruit that is divine;                    *Matthew 7:15-20
salt to flavor an age, so dull and bland,                *Matthew 5:13
and light that beckons from on a stand;              *Matthew 5:14-16

for the name of Christ, so reviled;                      *Matthew 5:11
but in love, with brothers, reconciled;               *Matthew 5:23-24

hungering...                                             *Matthew 5:6
for the Bread I crave,                                   *John 6:35
thirsting...                                             *Matthew 5:6
for Living Water's wave;                                 *John 4:4-26

watchful for this world's dark end,                      *Luke 21:34-36
and ready for Christ Who'll come again.            *Revelation 22:12-20

Despite my schemes,
and selfish dreams...
what if these seeds take root when sown—                 *Matthew 13:1-9
like daisies through cracks
can't be held back
by concrete once they've grown.

What if three commands
that God demands,
in spite of marks I've missed:

are to act justly;
love mercy;
walk humbly…                                                    *Micah 6:8
and what if that's the end of lists?

Is this enough for me,
and can I be satisfied
when glory waits
at Heaven's Gate
and acclaim I am denied?

LORD, help me be
all you would see
as humble and Your's alone…
and set apart
my wicked heart,                                          *Jeremiah 17:9
turn it to flesh – not stone.                           *Ezekiel 36:26

For when disciples grumbled,
and when they fought with strife
over who would be the greatest
among them all in paradise…        *Mark 9:33-37, Luke 9:46-48

You said it is the servant of all
who would sit with such esteem.
And no man, not one,                                    *Romans 3:10-12
save God's own Son
has served all and can redeem!              *2nd Corinthians 5:21

So God please take my every dream,
my every ill-spent whim…
and channel them into a passion
that strives only for Him.

Set apart is what I am to be,
and the only race I've left to run…              *Hebrews 12:1-2
is to see that Christ be glorified,
and for Him souls are won!

# WHAT IF...

What if every second,
incessant pain remains?
What if every moment
seems but another link in chains.

What if health is lost?
With jobs and sanity?
What if bills devour
and my children, I cannot feed?

What if prosperity
*...never comes...*
despite my wait?
What if poverty
is my elusive fate?

What if every goal I set
is failed
and I'm not Abel?                               *Genesis 4:3-4
What if in vain,
my hopes like Cain,
are dashed 'neath turning tables?    *Matthew 21:12, John 2:13-16

What if I'm rejected,
cast out,
among my peers?
What if I'm subject
to hate
and constant, goading jeers?

What if I loose
all that I've gained
and have nothing left to show?
What if all my fears,
*so dark—so near*
are justified and throw...

300   ◦   M. LEANNE TODD

my dream to winds
I cannot stay,
my honor to men
I cannot sway...

and all my hope is gone?
What then, say I, of Christ?
That He redeemed me
to a God,
Whose wrath and rod
would crush me neath its might.

What if I hear
I don't deserve
salvation, so highly priced?
What if I see
no good in me                                      *Romans 3:10
for which His grace sufficed?         *2 Corinthians 12:9-10

What if I know
that I was dead
but live,
because of Him?                                   *John 11:25-26
What if He never answers
every prayer of mine or whim?

Would I still love
the God He is...?
Would I still take up my cross?    *Matthew 16:24-26, Luke 9:23
I would for He,
was given for me,                                    *John 3:16
when I was shamed and lost!

# WHAT IS THIS SWEET AFFECTION?

What is this sweet affection...
I feel whenever near...                              *James 4:8
Your Word, oh God,
that falls on me—
that
I am
blessed
to hear?                                             *Matthew 13:16

What is this silent calm...
dawning o'er
the battles that I fight,                            *1 Timothy 6:12
like the sun standing still                          *Joshua 10:1-15
all at Your will
when Joshua prayed for light?

And what is this agony
in the depths of my despair...
like a panting deer                                  *Psalm 42:1
or silver, seared,                                   *Malachi 3:1-3
when it seems I haven't got a prayer?

What is this source compelling me,
calling me to turn more...
from sins, oh God,
which bind me                                        *John 8:34
from righteousness that I yearn for?                 *Matthew 5:6

Though I stumble                                     *Matthew 5:29-30
deep in it,
the sea of all my doubt,
I look to You
with faith renewed...
as bruised reeds,                                    *Isaiah 42:3
from seeds                                           *Genesis 22:15-18
that sprout.

And I know this: that You are God
and will hold me in Your hands...          *Psalm 145:14, Isaiah 41:10
for there my name is written                              *Isaiah 49:16
from before the ages
of stars and sands.                                    *Genesis 22:15-18

What is this sweet affection then...
stealing o'ver me through it all:
weaknesses,
insults,
distresses,
persecutions,
difficulties – large and small?                    *2 Corinthians 12:10

It is the strength that comes on High
when God does not turn His face...                    *Ezekiel 39:29
and emboldens us
in steadfast love.
It is His all-sufficient grace.                      *2 Corinthians 12:9

# WHAT OCCURRED TO ME MOST

It occurred to me,
that I'm not good enough                    *Romans 3:10
to ever even come close
to earning God's grace or love.         *Ephesians 2:8-9

It occurred to be,
that I'm not Abel;                              *Genesis 4:4
to rightly sit at
His marriage table.                     *Revelation 19:6-9

It occurred to me,
that I can't win
this race I've started                      *Hebrews 12:1
over even begin…

to be righteous enough
to make God proud,
no matter how long,
or lovely, or loud…

I sing His thanks
and morning praises—
I can only hope mine
are old bones He raises.                 *Ezekiel 37:1-14

It occurred to me
futile attempts at perfection
is not what orders
divine election.                   *John 15:16, 1 Peter 1:2

What occurred to me
is that I'm a dry cistern                    *Jeremiah 2:3
without His Word
with which to discern.

What occurred to me
is that I need to know more
of that Word flowing out
of the Bible that pours...

like a fountain of life                    *Isaiah 55:1, John 7:37-39
in my murky dead sea,
cleansing my soul
from all of sin's debris.

It occurred to me,
that I need to be less,
and God needs to be more
in my soul to be blessed.

For as quickly as
Scripture divides like a knife...          *Hebrews 4:12
what occurred to me most
is that I need the Christ.

# WHEN FAITH IS FOUND

Sometimes I feel just like a child,
left tossed by ocean waves...                    *Ephesians 4:14
blown by cold winds
the enemy                                        *1 Peter 5:8
sends;
apart from One Who saves.

Sometimes I feel just like a reed,               *Isaiah 42:3
so bruised from all I've heard,
that sways beneath the moving sea—
yet unbroken by His Word.

Sometimes I stumble,                             *2 Peter 1:10
captured,
in a thousand skeptic qualms...
that could be soothed
if it was proved
in Gilead, there's a Balm.                       *Jeremiah 8:22

Sometimes I feel so unsure,
so questioning and alone.
Yet despite the scare
I humbly dare
to come boldly 'fore the Throne...              *Hebrews 4:16

begging Christ to not
snuff out this smoldering wick,                  *Isaiah 42:3
this dying flame within.
Give it a spark,                                 *Romans 12:11
not miss the mark,
like all my other sins.

Dear LORD, You know my weakness,                 *2 Corinthians 12:9
my inward wordless groans.                       *Romans 8:26
Hear all them now

and show me how
You raise the old dry bones!                               *Ezekiel 37:1-14

For left inside the hollow
in my cave of dark and doubt,
I'm left there bare
– my spirit snare –
fearing there's no Way out.                                 *John 14:16

So let me cling onto the Vine                               *John 15:5
that You have sent,
reside in it;
abide in it;
til all my anger's spent.

Then in the clearing
I emerge,
content to cast my cares;                        *Psalm 55:22; 1 Peter 5:7
And by faith, not sight,                              *2 Corinthians 5:7
through the good fight…                                *1 Timothy 6:12
finding God
has answered prayers!

# WHEN IT COMES TO BEING JESUS

Some say that God is only love,
and only love He is,
from women in our churches
whose doctrine's hit or miss…

in pulpits where they ought not be
if God, they understand,
for Paul forbid a woman preach                      *1 Timothy 2:11-15
or hold authority over man.

Surely weeds have grown                        *Matthew 13:24-30
if truth be known—
but that we must keep hid,
lest it expose
the lies we've told
about the *love* of sin.

For what *is* Love?
And what is hate?
And how can they be measured?
For if we equate
rebuke                                          *2 Timothy 3:16-17
with hate…
we've lost sight of our treasure.                  *Matthew 13:44

It's buried now
in distant field
over grown with rot and moss,
but will be unearthed
with each rebirth                                      *John 3:1-3
and burning of the dross.                            *Malachi 3:1-3

For precious metals
can be restored
in a fire                                            *Hebrews 12:29

that's hot enough,
to demonstrate
what's truly hate
and what is truly love.

I'll tell you what love is
and how it can been seen!                    *Matthew 13:16
For Love was lifted up          *Numbers 21:4-9, John 3:14-21
when Christ drank the cup                    *Matthew 26:39
of
WRATH
'gainst you and me.

Yes, wrath, I say
and say again—
so we might bow in prayer
        o're the grievous state
for what
"God hates…"                                  *Proverbs 6:16-19
ALL OUR SIN
that put Christ there.

So lay aside your vain ideas
and hear                                      *Matthew 13:16
this truth be known…
that stars of night
don't shine as bright
when angels of light                          *2 Corinthians 11:14
are shone.

It's only through the darkness
when we
can see                                       *Matthew 13:16
the beacons of the sky;
just as it's only through godly sorrow        *2 Corinthians 7:10
that we
can see                                       *Matthew 13:16
the grace of God, Most High.

It's only then we value
a pearl                                          *Matthew 13:44-45
of some great price,
and not some jewels
or gold of fools,
who do not know the Christ.

For what is wisdom's true beginning,
as Solomon claimed—
but the FEAR of God above,                       *Proverbs 9:10
and what is gauged
as war is waged
with sin, assuaged,
I'll tell you—that's not love.

For Love is selfless,
fearing not,
the slings and bows of words...
that call us
hypocrites and haters
when egos, we have stirred.

So don't palate people in their sin
that separates them from God,
or you might be
as a fallen star                        *Isaiah 14:12-14, Luke 10:8
of the morning
'neath His rod.

Yes, what was God but a burning bush...?     *Exodus, Chapter 3
And His presence a holy ground...?
What was God but a blinding light
crushing Paul from a horse top, down...?         *Acts 9:1-16

Again, what's wisdom...?
as Solomon declared;
and what makes it grand, but simple?
But the FEAR of the LORD

Who whipped with cords                    *Matthew 21:12, John 2:13-17
money-changers in the temple!

And what is holy?
Surely not our hearts
so deceitfully wicked, sick, ill-led…                    *Jeremiah 17:9
which would dare ask us
on our road to Damascus
"Surely…hath God said?"                              *Genesis 3:1

We are no judge of what is good.                      *Romans 3:10
We are no judge of charity…
when we bow
to sacred cows                              *Exodus, Chapter 32
of feelings, friends, sincerity.

So we must lean upon God's Word                      *Proverbs 3:5-6
for the sake of those Christ saves,
and not on
good intentions
with which the road to hell is paved.

Though God is there
for casting cares,                                  *1 Peter 5:7
He is not there to please us.
And Jesus doesn't need "our help"          *2 Sam 6:3-8, 1 Chr 13:7-11
when it comes to being Jesus.

# WHEN LIGHTNING COMES

When lightning cracks
it splits the black
      of night into small fractions.
It's aim lets us find
our sight from the blind
      and sparks a call to action.

Crisp volts from Heaven
pierced                         *Isaiah 53:5, John 19:34
      seventy times seven,           *Matthew 18:22
      at last—it makes connection
with a true conduit
gentle and fluid,
      living water                   *John 7:38
      will pose no rejection.

Then energy streaks
through seas and creeks
      as the body of water
         comes *alive*.           *1 Corinthians 15:22
And passing strangers
imagine a danger
      from being touched
         by the tide.

That water, thought weak,
though still supple and meek
      becomes a force beyond measure.
With no shape of its own
now it has grown
      to house the most powerful treasure.

But wood is so dense           *Deuteronomy 28:36
-tightly packed, takes offense-
      and offers the lightning

no room…                                    *Luke 2:7
wood poses a barrier
and won't be a carrier
        for the only source
        to break the gloom.

And lightning will undo
what it can't
get through to—
        rough barks, bitter limbs are to blame.
So when lightning hits,
wood splinters a bit,
        before it ignites into flame.

That strong and dense wood
that once loomed and stood
        on it's on muddied ground and rich grass,
will fall
        in a crash
to be smothered in ash
        like remains from a house
                made of glass.

So true strength is deceptive
when we are receptive
        to the lightning's bright rapid pace,
in the comforting rod                        *Psalm 23:4
that comes from our, God,
        in the form of His swift, soothing grace.    *Hebrews 4:16

# WHEN TRUTH OFFENDS

A thorn bush grew                                        *Judges 9:7-20
so we named it king.
It offered no shade
but songs, it could sing.

And that was enough
to sway us indeed,
like little mice
        dancing off
                through the weeds...          *Matthew 13:24-30

...and into a ditch                              *Matthew 15:14
blind mice, such as we
did stumble                      *Matthew 5:29-30, Mark 9:43-45
into an abyss                                    *Revelation 9:11
        and dead sea.

And all the king's horses
and all the king's men
could never save us
from all the king's sin.

But we'll defend
those thorns til the end,
as standards bend
when Truth                                            *John 14:6
offends.

# WHEN YOU CAME ALONG
-A Poem for my Kids

When you were weak,
I had to be strong.
When you were lost,
I made you belong.

When you were hurting,
I eased your pain.
When you were dirty,
I washed every stain.

When you were hungry,
I made sure to feed.
When you wanted,
I fulfilled every need.

When you were scared,
I calmed your fear.
When you were crying,
I wiped every tear.

But when I was hateful,
so jaded and wrong…
like a light in the dark,
that's when you came along.

When days felt so pointless
in every season,
you became
my purpose, my mission, my reason.

When dreams seemed hopeless,
so barren and bland,
you made them come true…
far better than planned.

When I was broken,
you made me whole,
with sweet smiles and giggles
that brightened my soul.

For these things and more
I will keep doing what I do,
because it's so clear to me…
just who's restored who.

# WHO IS THIS ANCIENT CARPENTER?

Who is this ancient carpenter            *Matthew 13:54-55
in whom I must believe?                   *John 3:16
Will he forgive these doubts,
and my shameful soul receive?

What is this aged text,
I cling to in the night?
What are its profound meanings,
cloaked in mysteries and in might?

How can I hold on to its truth              *John 14:6
while the world pulls me from it—
like tossing waves          *Ephesians 4:14, James 1:6
that cannot save
as I coat my pain and numb it?

Because there are so many
obstacles,
just lying
in my path...
will I be called a faithful servant,       *Matthew 25:23
or invoke all of God's wrath?           *John 3:36

Who is this lowly Spirit           *Matthew 11:29
that never leaves my side?         *Matthew 28:20
Whose tender tone,
from a mighty throne,
now calls me to decide?

I sought Him in the struggles
and for decades chased His Ghost.
I've praised Him in silent victories,
of which I cannot boast.          *Ephesians 2:8-9

So much is complicated.
So little, I ascertain.
But words in red                              *Matthew 24:35
have not been said
to my sickened heart in vain.                  *Jeremiah 17:9

I'll ask the ancient carpenter.
I'll seek the truth He gives.
I'll knock that doors be opened,               *Matthew 7:7-8
so I rise to truly live.                        *Romans 6:4

# WISDOM IN THE STORM

Where are my words of wisdom now?
Are there blessings God's been disguising?
When hope is dim
when we can't swim…
with dark skies and water rising?

What am I to make of this—
when toward doubt I am inclining?
What is left
inside this cleft
when clouds hold no silver lining?

What do I do when thunder rumbles,
heralding yet more storm…
and lightning strikes
of which the likes
divide my marrow's form?

A siren's shriek—
EMERGENCY!
Lights out and power's gone.
I chide myself
having not seen wealth
in countless past bright dawns…

unlike this one that's masked in gray,
its tears in driving sheets of rain—
trapping us in rooms,
turning homes to tombs;
while nerves spin with weather vanes.

Where are my words of wisdom now?
Yes, those I surely lack…
while the adversary
longs to carry
my soul in faith's grim fade to black.

Where are my words of wisdom now
when my heel can't crush the head...
of this cunning asp,                                    *Genesis 3:15
who my weakness—clasped,
I'll turn to Christ instead.


Who tells me through the fear of God                    *Proverb 9:10
I could be quite the sage,
who tells me He is with us
until the very end of age.                              *Matthew 28:20


Who is the Calmer of all seas,     *Matthew 8:23-27, Mark 4:35-41
depicted in windows, stained...
whose Word is hidden                                    *Psalm 119:11
neath my breast
in a strong, beating refrain.


For what is wisdom...?
It's beginning, its value, or its worth?
It's the fear of the LORD
that strikes a cord
igniting our soul's rebirth!                            *John 3:1-13


So rise in me,
Dear Word of God!
Waken whispers that
still are calling...
be the victor of my soul
despite my state so weak and fallen!


You said when storms and winds will beat...
You said a house remains;                               *Matthew 7:24-27
if on the Cornerstone
it's mount;
and a fount                                    *Isaiah 55:1, John 37: 37-39
will us, sustain!

And so, dear God...I cry to You,
despite these dismal waves;
knowing Hope's alive
and by Your side,                                    *Hebrews 1:13
wisdom's knowing
the One who saves!                                    *Acts 4:9-12

Yes, words of wisdom,
I seek and find;                                      *Matthew 7:7-8
yes, words of wisdom grand...
as floods devour,
let demons cower,
for I've a Rock on which to stand.                    *Psalm 18:2

# WORDS IN RED

Someone said the words in red,
Someone said the words in red

now they've always been—                          *John 1:1
and will always be,                          *Matthew 24:35
but as far as
most mortal eyes
can see:                                     *Matthew 13:16

before a word originates
whether it
        breeds love or hate
it must be whispered
thought or said
        though it's not so with words in red

but we cannot say, *they don't exist*
in all the pews—on book store lists

from hills to valleys, everywhere
the words in red make us aware

though opinions, we're entitled to
we can't deny one thing is true:

that Someone said the words in red
as many saw
His blood was shed            *Mark 15:24, Luke 23:33, John 19:18
and Someone *said* the words in red

words seldom come out of thin air
words can't convict our sins out there

words, when used as a tool of man,
can't always dowse the flames they fan

words can disguise and can conceal
wounds only words in red can heal

for words in red have Life to give                    *John 14:6
and they will forever live          *Matthew 24:35, Mark 13:31

our words may come and they may go
like kingdoms, cancers, fads, or snow

but keep this simple, so we know
how to avoid the undertow

for waves of words are rushing by
leaving some
        behind to die
and on those, we can't rely—
let words in red
        lift us
            up high...

to walk on waters deep with dread              *Matthew 14:29
to trample them neath heels instead              *Genesis 3:15

to die with them                                    *1 Peter 2:24
and bring to Life
His purpose, passion, plan, and wife           *Revelation 19:7

but in the mean time, we can tarry
spin our wheels until we're wary:

dispute if He was rich or poor
dispute if He *had loved* a whore
dispute if He was meek or vain
dispute if He was mad or sane
dispute if He was bred and born
dispute if He was sometimes torn
dispute if He resisted sin
dispute if He will come again

dispute if He was weak or strong
dispute if to Him, you belong

but we can't dispute The Gospel, read
for
**it is written**
and souls are led

duck or dodge them, here today
as prophets preach them, come what may

for JESUS
said those words in red
they have been published, pressed, and spread

passed the test, and fit to print
into all nations, they'll be sent

and you may doubt
or you may dread…
but
*know you're LOVED*                                 *John 3:16
by Whom they're said

# SALVATION STORY

I stood there in the pews, head bowed – not in prayer, but in anguish. I was standing, pensively, in a small little southern Baptist church with a new young preacher, who was on fire for the Gospel, and laying out his alter call.

But I wouldn't budge. Stubborn little prideful mule I was at the age of 14 or so. Yes – there were many things that pride would not permit.

Besides all of which, the anger over my parent's dissolving marriage had settled into me like some sort of alien sickness. And despite their lip service to Jesus, I could scarcely recall a time when I had been taken to any church as a small child. Of course our lovely home was cluttered with little religious plaques and symbols, along with the occasional and woefully ignorant, unbiblical *opinions* that my parents had tossed around about the Christ in front of me... but when such an atmosphere is also coupled with fury, profanities, pornography, substance abuse and a near total lack of love for one another...well, it can make a child quite jaded about the existence and involvement of any god – much less, the only real One.

And so, there I was – standing, solumnly, in the pews. *Why?* I asked unconsciously with every refusal to move, *why were my parents suffering – why was I?* Sure my grandmother had once sat me on her knee, telling me stories of how this Messiah had turned the water into wine, how He had raised the dead, and how He had died Himself for the sins of all the world. So if He was so amazingly capable, why was there such misery, not just in my own little life, but in the whole world at large? Frankly, in my estimation at the time, if He existed at all then He must be quite the divine Jerk for allowing it.

No, it wasn't so much that I didn't believe in God, as it was the fact that I was *mad at Him.*

Then breaking into my wall of resistance, the pastor added suddenly...but softly, "I feel the person whom the LORD is calling today *is* a youth."

My heart quickened.

*Really, Padre?* I remember thinking, *Well then – male or female? You'll have to be more specific than that if you expect ME to humiliate myself!*

Clearly, I wasn't into parlor tricks and psycho babble. This gentleman was going to have to do better than that if he expected me to embarrass myself in front of all these people.

Eventually, they closed the service. And a myriad of mixed emotions hit me. At first I was relieved. After all, I was off the hook now. But soon that relief caved into a sinking feeling that I had forsaken something, or Someone, far greater than I could ever imagine; Someone I didn't even know or understand...at least, not yet.

*Next week, God.* I bargained with the Almighty. *I'll go down during next week's alter call.*

But that is when I learned something about this Yahweh. And that is that He would not be "put off."

As I waited on the porch steps of the church for my brother and new sister-in-law to get their vehicle, I heard my name being called. I turned and – to my horror – it was the pastor himself. I dreaded any interaction with him. I suddenly felt like some undesirable vagrant who was caught trespassing on a rich man's property, like I didn't belong – or so I was led to believe, momentarily. Fearing reproach and certain judgment, I somehow summoned the courage to look this man in the eye.

And that's when I was quite surprised. His eyes were not cold and distant or disapproving – but bright and loving. He did not sneer at me for being such a lowly sinner, but smiled such a welcoming smile that I was captivated, drunk in the love that seem to exude from him so effortlessly. Whatever was flowing out of this man who grinned affectionately at me, all I knew at the time was that I flatly didn't deserve it.

And yet there it was: Grace. Mercy. Love.

He said, "Leanne...I felt like *you* were the person the LORD was calling today. And I just felt that He wanted me to give you this."

It was the New Testament.

I don't even remember what, if anything, I said in response. My jaw had dropped, spiritually. *Male or female..?* I had challenged this man. Umm...yea.

One thing was for certain. This guy didn't play. I wasn't invited to "Popcorn and Movie Night" for months and years on end in the vain hope that some of this "Christianity stuff" would rub off on me. I was not "entertained." And I reasoned, that if this man had the gumption to hit me sidelong with the truth like that, the least I could do was read what he gave me.

And that I did. I don't remember how many of the four Gospels I had read before the Spirit of our Holy God made me understand that He is not cold and distant and condemning, but that His mercies are new everyday. That once we come to Christ when we are called, our sin is blotted out and we are given a clean slate. That this Jesus, is the Living Embodiment of Yahweh...in all His hard truth, yet amazing grace.

Do you know Him today? If not, then I say FIND. SEEK. Knock, and His door will be opened with so much grace that you will drown in it. You will die, yes, you but you will also come to *life!*

# THE BIRD MAN

A Short Story dedicated to my late father,
Alvie Lee Whistler

My father's hair was shaved, and fifty silver staples pierced the side of his head. His legs, deformed since childhood, accentuated his frailty. "A hemorrhagic stroke..." doctors recanted, "...spilled blood into the brain...the catheter will drain the excess fluid to stop the brain from swelling – any further..." Their silence was more comforting than their play-by-play commentary. And in that delicate moment the enemy spoke through a favorite form—someone with good intentions. "...maybe God gave your Daddy this stroke to get you to move back home."

I wasn't upset with the person. She had no idea what possessed her to say that, just as I had no idea how to combat it. But that comment was the tip of the iceberg to my mountain of guilt. Years ago, my husband and I had moved away with the military, eventually settling on the east coast, far away from our childhood homes. Phone calls were the only way to bridge the distance with my dad. In our talks I could hear the happy chatter of Dad's parakeets. They offered motion and sound in his small apartment. My brother and his family were always there for our dad, inviting him to ball games and holidays. But I wasn't. And these chattering, tiny creatures were a subtle reminder that my father relied on birds, instead of my children, for his daily joy and companionship.

Watching his chest heave in time with the breathing machine, I decided not return to Maryland. Many obstacles stood in the way—our deep financial debt, our mortgage, our new pregnancy, and my husband's urgent warning that the economy wasn't stable in my home town. But I wouldn't listen. I wanted to stay with my father, so he wouldn't have to live in a nursing home. Everyone assumed his Medicare and Medicaid would cover the cost of in-home nurses. We could rent our house in Maryland state, and work opposite shifts in odd jobs until a better job came along in Dallas. But I could be there. It could work. Such was my hope.

Though seemingly unconscious, my father would respond to certain commands, like squeezing our hands when asked. But he suddenly he stopped responding to anyone or anything. The hospital staff never volunteered the word "coma" to describe his condition, until pinned for a direct answer. He had a feeding tube, a tracheotomy, and a catheter. Under the stipulations of his Medicare and Medicaid, he couldn't return home until he was "...down to only one tube." So at the time of his discharge, a nursing home was our only choice—for the short run, I had hoped.

Gradually, he began to come around. But he was now paralyzed on his entire left side. For the remainder of his life, he would be confined to a bed and wheelchair, completely dependent on others to survive. As a child, a bone disease destroyed my father's hip joint, causing a permanent disability. But he learned how to use crutches, and nothing could stop him. He cleaned house for his mother, and ran races in school. He would even mediate squabbles between his siblings—one stout toss of a crutch in their direction would settle most disputes. He'd been a draftsman, and had a fascination with turning old pieces of scrap iron into beautiful sculptures. He'd drop his crutches, scale a ladder, light his torch, and start to weld. At those times, I witnessed my father bending iron by his sheer force of will. So it was unthinkable, that such a fiercely independent soul would have to be bound now by bed sheets and circumstance. We met him with smiles in the desperate hope that if we seemed happy, he might not feel so bad. The arm that had once melted iron would tremble from under the blankets, like the helpless flutter of some wild creature —now caged.

And we soon faced another horrible truth. More often than not, he didn't recognize us, and was seldom aware of his true surroundings. His wry grin and twinkling eyes had been replaced by an expressionless, haunting stare. He would ask for his crutches repeatedly, forgetting that he was paralyzed. He would ask for food he could not eat and water he could not drink. On all three counts, we were told to deny him.

Perhaps what disturbed me the most was when he would also ask about deceased relatives, as if they were still with us. His questions always centered around the prospect of going to see them. For some mysterious reason, he was under the impression that they were accessible to him now. And I wondered if perhaps they had been for a time, given his recent experiences. They were foremost on his mind, moreso than us.

Missing my father had always been hard while living states away, but it was harder still to miss him while holding his hand. Often I would leave the parking lot of the nursing home screaming obscenities and smashing my fists into the dashboard.

Much like Jacob, my father had spent a life time of *wrestling* with God. So many unhealthy dreams and aspirations often plagued his walk with Christ, ultimately bringing him to a place of destitution and isolation. One by one, the Almighty had hand plucked each and every little idol in my father's life away, quite simply and systematically...because ultimately, I believe, he belonged to God. And the last of these obsessions, was with alcohol.

When I was a child, my father used to tell the story of the little lamb held by Jesus in a famous portrait. In my father's tale, the little lamb would often stray. And so, to keep the little lamb from straying into a pack of wolves or over a cliff to its own peril, the Good Shepherd would hobble this particular wayward lamb.

"The Shepherd would take his rod, and he would break that lamb's legs," my father would explain to me. "But after the Shepherd broke its leg, the Shepherd would then carry the little lamb and raise him up. He would love the lamb and take care of it. And after a time, that little lamb would learn that all he ever really needed came from the Shepherd anyway. And the lamb would no longer stray."

Stripped, like Job, of everything by his late sixties, my father had only his drink left. And I wondered if the LORD had allowed this stroke in order to put my father in a position where he could no longer sin with excessive alcohol, thus removing the very last idol from his life.

But what ever the divine rhyme or reason to this horrific situation, soon other worries surfaced. Our house hadn't rented soon enough, and we faced foreclosure. The only available jobs did not keep us off food stamps or out of bankruptcy. Now four months pregnant, I contacted viral pneumonia. Then medical tests indicated that our new baby might have Downs Syndrome. That news came as quite a blow, since one of our children is severely affected by Autism. Could we manage another disability? And every time I visited my father, he would look me right in my eyes and ask, "Where's Leanne?" I would fight back a tear, gently pat his leg that still had feeling, and tell him hoarsely, "I'm Leanne, Dad. I'm right here."

In those darkest hours, the enemy would ask me where my God was. After all, I had "honored my father..." and had "taken a leap of faith..." so, where was He? After a while, the argument became convincing. So I screamed aloud at God one day. I told Him, quite frankly, that if all of this was part of His plan, then in my opinion His 'plan' SUCKED.

The still small whisper we know to be the Holy Spirit made me consider Christ and His suffering on the cross – a notion that I interrupted by yelling, "And why did JESUS have to go through all of THAT?! Why is there such misery?! YOU TELL ME WHY!!!"

But as is the case with any gentle natured Dove, too much ranting noise had made Him flutter smooth-cool AWAY. And there I was, left in the absence of God: a blank abyss with no meaning, reason, or hope. Life was just a time-killer. I cried face down, stinging tears into the carpet. I considered a life without God. What would it be like to gaze into the sunlit edges of a cloud and feel only the dreaded heat of another summer day? What would it be like not to feel His eminence and humble glory in the face of the sky? I could not imagine it. Even though I was still angry and confused, I resolved that I could not live without Him because of all His attributes—He is hope.

Then in my silence, gentle notions came to me. Faith is more than a belief—it is the very way through which we communicate with Christ. And without that, how can we expect Him to respond? That's like hanging up the phone on a trusted Friend then getting angry because He's not listening or answering our questions. Next I remembered the doctors explanations, "Frequent smoking and excessive alcohol can bring on a stroke." This suggestion was part of the doctor's sideline commentary that had been "less-comforting" for me to hear at the time. So for decades my dad had laid the groundwork for this situation. The stroke was not a *punishment* for sinning with alcohol, but was rather the simple physical consequence of prolonged unhealthy habits that God was now using to set my father apart in holiness.

And had *God* asked me to take my leap of faith, or had I been trying to enact my own will, assuming that it was His? Is it fair to jump off a cliff, and blame God when we hit the ground? These little revelations replaced my tears, coming not as criticisms, but as comfort. How amazing is such grace?

Three days later, my brother's church gave us a baby shower. A congregation who'd never met us donated endless baby supplies and a mountain of groceries. Family and friends brought gifts. And my aunt suddenly gave us several thousand dollars, just because she knew we'd been out of work. These acts of kindness converged in one weekend, after my decision to keep trusting God. Even during my doubts, the LORD was prompting people to help us. And blessings continued. My husband found work. And a more promising job was later offered in another part of the state.

That posed a painful decision—staying in town meant staying on food stamps, perhaps indefinitely. Welfare had been a temporary means to an end, but we couldn't let it become a legacy for our children. Many obstacles hindered our move back to Texas, like road blocks I chose to ignore. But now circumstances fell right in line. It was like a way had been made through effortless forces, and we were compelled to follow.

Over the next year, we made regular trips to see my dad. During this time, he had recurrent episodes of pneumonia. In late August of 2006, his heart rate failed during CPR in his final bout with that disease. I was not there when he died. In spite of our efforts over the last three years, I had failed him one last time.

The funeral home was flooded with all of my father's old acquaintances. His housekeepers also came to see him, telling me, "Oh, we had to come see the Bird Man! That's what we called him! You know your daddy loved his birds!" Another man commented, "The old Alvie had more lives than a cat!" Their presence was yet another blessing. Their jovial nature and bright smiles reminded me that God's joy was still alive, and therefore, could return to us again someday.

And that same joy was with the pastor at the funeral. He was not sad, nor was he solemn. Instead, he had a smile a mile wide. His eyes were on fire with the brightest light, and he would give the devil no room. He told us,

"...I lived in a lot of houses. Some were shabby, and some were nice—but I've never lived in a house that is completely made of gold. Alvie Whistler has, though. He's been there since Tuesday." And that's when I realized that my dad now sees everything in a newly restored mind. He sees my efforts—that I had, for once, put him first—for as long as I possibly could have.

Days later my sister-in-law had a dream. It is common knowledge in our family, that her dreams are oddly prophetic in nature. This time she saw our dad walking, completely upright, as tall as any other man. He was content, unaware of anyone and unconcerned about anything—with no crutches, tubes, tracheotomies, or staples. As an eagle who mounts up on wings to soar, our father now walks in a new found freedom that's been granted by the *grace* of a Dove.

www.ingramcontent.com/pod-product-compliance
Lightning Source LLC
Chambersburg PA
CBHW071707120626
46550CB00001B/133